Also by Diane Irons

THE WORLD'S BEST-KEPT BEAUTY SECRETS

THE WORLD'S BEST-KEPT DIET SECRETS

911
BEAUTY SECRETS

An Emergency Guide to Looking Great at Every Age, Size and Budget

DIANE IRONS

Sourcebooks, Inc.®
Naperville, IL

Published by Sourcebooks, Inc.
P.O. Box 372
Naperville, IL 60566
630.961.3900
Fax: 630.961.2168

ISBN 0-7394-0674-4
Printed and bound in the United States of America

TABLE OF CONTENTS

ACKNOWLEDGMENTS   vii

INTRODUCTION   viii

Chapter 1   ATTITUDE ADJUSTMENTS   01

Chapter 2   SUPER SKIN   15

Chapter 3   HAND & NAIL HELP   39

Chapter 4   FABULOUS FEET   47

Chapter 5   INTIMATE INSPIRATIONS   53

Chapter 6   INSIDE/OUT BEAUTY   79

Chapter 7   QUICK FACES   99

Chapter 8   HAPPY HAIR   123

Chapter 9   STYLE SENSE   149

Chapter 10   WORKING STYLE   165

Chapter 11   SPECIAL OCCASIONS   173

Chapter 12   WONDERFUL WEDDINGS   183

Chapter 13   PREGNANCY CHALLENGES   191

Chapter 14   SEASONAL BEAUTY   197

Chapter 15   ACCESSORIES   211

Chapter 16   GETTING ORGANIZED   223

Chapter 17   CARE & MAINTENANCE   229

Chapter 18   BODY BEAUTIFUL   237

Chapter 19   FIGURE FLATTERY   251

Chapter 20   MODELS & CELEBRITIES   263

Chapter 21   FAST-LANE BEAUTY   269

Chapter 22   BEAUTY ON A BUDGET   275

Chapter 23   BEAUTY ON THE ROAD   281

Chapter 24   ILLNESS EMERGENCIES   285

Chapter 25   COSMETIC QUICK FIXES   293

Chapter 26   EMERGENCY DIETS   303

BEFORE I LEAVE YOU   311

INDEX   313

ABOUT THE AUTHOR   325

ACKNOWLEDGMENTS

Thanks to my family, friends, and colleagues who have supported my mission to demystify beauty and fitness.

I would especially like to thank Laureen Flanagan for graciously hosting focus groups to allow me to better understand women's views on beauty as a lifestyle choice.

Thanks to those "forever" friends from Peabody High School. You are all beautiful, inside and out!

My deep gratitude to my friends and colleagues at Sourcebooks for their incredible enthusiasm and patience.

INTRODUCTION

In the thirty-five years I have been involved in the beauty industry, I have seen just about every beauty crisis that's known to woman. Many times, I have been called upon to solve these problems, and most often, time is of the essence. "Diane, you've got twenty minutes to make our star look twenty pounds thinner." That's an easy one. "Hey, Di, Ms. Celebrity didn't get that face lift. Get some years off her face!" Okay, just tell me how many years off you need, and I'll let you know how long it will take. These beauty alarms happen behind those runways, on movie sets, and on TV shows, but they also happen in everyday living.

"Help! I am going to meet my ex, and need to lose ten pounds in a week—or at least look like I have!"

"Yikes, I'm going on a big date, and a giant zit has taken over my face!"

"Oh no! I just colored my hair, and now it's bright orange!"

I've seen these emergencies and so much worse. I've solved most of them, and I'm here to solve yours. I hope you'll use these tips not only to solve those beauty issues, but to streamline your own beauty routines, add some glamour to your life, share your beauty finds with your friends, daughters, mothers, colleagues, and save a lot of money and frustration.

Until now, when your do-it-yourself hair dye turned orange or purple, you'd end up calling your hair stylist, which takes time and money and defeats the purpose of doing it yourself.

Or you'd try desperately to cover up that pimple, and look like you're wearing a giant "bump" on your face.

Beauty myths abound. Besides solving your problems, I hope to bring practicality to your beauty care. We have every right to make beauty a part of our lives. We live in a world where first impressions are most lasting. But trust me, once you simplify your beauty, it will bring you confidence and contentment that will spill over into other parts of your life. Once you give yourself that respect, you'll be able to give to others. It will become an integral part of your well-being. Your new routines will become as natural and important to you as brushing your teeth. Becoming the best you can be—no matter what your size, age, or other parameters—is your birthright. Use it well.

Chapter 1

ATTITUDE ADJUSTMENTS

ATTITUDE 911

Attitude is the most important, cheapest, most life-changing beauty secret. It's the quickest fix I know. It beats out any product you can buy. It has the power to transform more dramatically than a "state of the art" haircut by the most sought-after hairstylist, or a makeover by a celebrated makeup artist.

I recently appeared on the *Maury Povich Show* in an effort to help teenage girls who felt too ugly to leave the house. These were all beautiful young women. There were two who had minor weight problems which they felt they were unable to combat because of their low self-esteem. The others had no real physical issues, but had been injured by unkind treatment by classmates. Which leads me to this chapter. All roads to beauty have to begin with the right attitude.

But what is attitude? These young women on the show told me how remarks made by others caused them to feel worse about themselves. Unfortunate as any unkind remark can be, it's the target that makes the difference. Send that remark to a young woman with strong self-esteem, with a positive attitude about herself, and it falls right off. It won't penetrate at all. A strong woman feels good about herself and believes that she is the center of the universe. Nothing and no one person can take those feelings away.

SELF-RESPECT

VISUALIZATION

If you truly want to change your looks, you need to visualize the specific changes. What will any improvements you make look like? See yourself with clearer skin, a streamlined body, shiny, healthier hair, majestic posture. These changes are realistic and attainable. Stay away from goals that you'll never reach. If you've never been a size 2, don't sabotage yourself by trying to get there. Don't compare yourself with someone you've seen on the cover of a magazine or on a TV or movie screen. Accept your uniqueness and capitalize on it.

MIRRORS BOOST ATTITUDE

The quickest attitude adjustment is through reflection. Women who struggle with esteem issues often tell me that they avoid mirrors like the plague. I suppose the rationale is "don't get yourself deeper into depression," but mirrors can become your biggest ally. They can tell you how you're progressing, in those little ways that may not be noticeable to the casual eye. Mirrors are the ultimate objective eye.

"I keep a full-length mirror by my back door. I use it to take a final glimpse of everything from my hem line to my posture. It is placed in rather strong but natural lighting so that I make sure my makeup is properly blended."
Victoria, 33

DO EVERYTHING BETTER

From washing your hair to applying moisturizer, the way you use your products will make all the difference in the final result. For instance, if you warm your facial moisturizer in your hands before application, it will go on smoothly. Try to duplicate what you see and feel when your hair is shampooed at a salon. You'll notice that product is always handled, never poured directly on the hair. Add a massage to your scalp when washing. While rinsing, lift your hair away from your scalp for about two minutes until it squeaks.

DISCOVER THE VIRTUES OF VANITY

When we were young, we experimented with our doll's hair, or if you were like me, created unimaginable hairdos on our younger sisters. We snuck our mother's makeup and played with her jewelry, perfume, shoes, and clothing. Confident women enjoy primping and experimenting as a way of relieving stress and boosting morale. Women who care about how they look are fascinating to watch, and teach us about taste, style, and glamour. I believe vanity is a positive virtue, allowing us to fix our heads as well as our looks.

SHOW OFF A LITTLE

OK, so we all know there is no such thing as the perfect body. Stop moaning and complaining about what's wrong with your own body and focus on what's right. If your butt is sagging, then show off your arms or calves. You are in control of what you show the world. Pick out your finest and flaunt it.

DON'T WORRY ABOUT LOOKING PRETTY—LOOK PRETTY AMAZING

Show the world you care about yourself. Real beauty celebrates individuality. Rather than running around looking for beauty in pricey external products, discover it within yourself. Make the most of what you have been given. You'll learn to like yourself, and that will spark a light from within.

DON'T FORGET THE DETAILS

If you're wearing a great dress with sexy heels, what good is it if your hair is dull and flat and your makeup is lackluster? Or your nails are chipped. How about sexy sandals on feet with corns and callouses? Spend the money or do it yourself, but don't overlook the finer points. Attention to details on the outside flaunts inner confidence and shows you care about yourself.

DO ONE THING FOR YOURSELF EVERY DAY

It's the ultimate act of self-respect. Make yourself do it. Read an inspiring book, soak in a bubble bath. It's these little pleasures that will allow you to feel special. Fake it if you must, until you actually feel deserving of it. Acting as if something is true can make it so. Whatever you choose, follow the action by writing down what you did and how it made you feel. Keep a journal and review it regularly. Make it your own "attitude file." Include stories, quotes from friends, and photos that have made you feel especially good about yourself.

ACT "AS IF"

What if you reached your ideal weight, stopped smoking, started exercising, and got your hair cut, how would your life be different? How would you feel? How would you act? Start acting that way today.

PROJECT BEAUTY

If you're feeling ugly, that's the persona people will see. Feel good, feel pretty, and that's just what the world will see. Try to look as good as you can, and then forget it. I've seen women who don't care if they have spinach in their teeth while others I've known can't go ten minutes without checking themselves out in a mirror. There's a happy medium somewhere in between. There are ways to live in beauty without being obsessive about it.

HEAR A POSITIVE ATTITUDE

FIND SUPPORTIVE FRIENDS

Whether intentional or not, what people say can make us feel good or bad about ourselves. Look for people, or maybe just that one person, who will make you feel good when you're feeling low. This person will give you unasked-for compliments. If you've done something different, if you're wearing something new, they'll notice. Collect these compliments and wear them. They are yours, and they will build your esteem.

"I call my sister whenever I am having a 'fat' or 'ugly' day. She tells me I'm beautiful, and we have a couple of laughs. Her support and perspective help me put my beauty crises to rest."
Jenny, 38

IGNORE BEAUTY BASHERS

There's no shame in wanting to look and feel your best. Magazines, cosmetic manufacturers, and the diet industry are not inherently evil, and not all beautiful models and actresses have eating disorders or drug addictions. Appearance still matters. Furthermore, caring for yourself physically will make you feel good emotionally. Treat yourself with respect, and you are far less likely to let anyone else treat you badly. The smartest ways to beauty are exercise and proper nutrition, which also provide important health benefits.

LISTEN TO YOUR INNER VOICE

Each of us has a voice inside our head that will give us advice. This voice is like a therapist. It will guide us in the right direction. It will calm us down, cheer us up, and even help us figure out why we're overeating or not bothering to iron our clothes. The problem is that we often don't take the quiet time we need to hear this important information. Schedule some quiet time in a leisurely bath or walk, or even while putting on your makeup. Treat this intuition as an inner cheering section.

OBSERVE

There's some great TV shows out there that feature women with attitude. My particular all-time favorite is *Absolutely Fabulous*, a British comedy. Although no longer in production, it can often be seen on Comedy Central. It's parody at its finest, and it pokes fun at the whole fashion biz, which takes itself much too seriously. I also recommend *Style* on CNN for its fashion literacy, and some of the fashion shows on E! Entertainment Television. Unfortunately, there's not much to watch in prime time on a regular basis. However, *Veronica's Closet* has an edge, as does *Just Shoot Me*.

SIMPLIFY

MAKE TIME

Even if it's just ten minutes a day, you must put aside the time to get yourself together. Use this time to try a different beauty routine, or to express your thoughts in a daily journal. Many women feel guilty about taking even a small amount of time for themselves, but you shouldn't feel that way. You will find yourself more willing and able to give to others once you learn to give to yourself.

STREAMLINE

When beauty is presented to us in the high-gloss fashion magazines, it seems overwhelming to the average woman. They dictate color, "must-haves" of the moment, and complicated, expensive regimes that would lead us to believe at least half our day and paychecks should be dedicated to the pursuit of perfection. Streamlining beauty routines makes sense to our busy lives. Products that perform more than one purpose, and clothing that goes from season to season, year after year, will allow you to be as spectacular as you want to be without the constraints of time or money.

TAKE A BREAK

At least twice a day, set aside five minutes to recheck your makeup, hair, posture, and clothing. No matter how impeccably you started out your day, a touch-up is both necessary and warranted. Take some deep breaths to renew and restore your appearance.

DO A LITTLE HOUSECLEANING

Getting rid of what makes you feel less than fabulous is vital to self-acceptance. Go through your closet and toss out anything that doesn't make you feel great about your body. Go through your makeup drawers and get rid of those less-than-flattering colors.

LIVE IN BEAUTY

Even if it's just a corner of a room, you should have an area that is dedicated to beauty. Make a routine that will allow you to get yourself together without effort. You'll be amazed at the difference it will make in your life. You'll feel more organized, appear more confident, and people will notice the change.

STYLE

DEVELOP A STYLE

What exactly is style? Although it means different things to different people, and it would take forever to debate what makes a person stylish, it comes down to what suits you. It is the look of confidence that shines through your clothing.

Everyone should have a style that's all their own. Yes, it's important to stay up-to-date on what's trendy. Then take those trends and adapt them to your own style. Never do the reverse. If you already have a style that's not sending out the right message, don't be afraid to change it. Just go for it. Change the way you look and see what the response is. Once you find a look that really works well for you, keep it. Use it from morning through evening with slight modifications.

"I finally got my look 'right' after years of trial and error. I am a casual person, and when I attempted to stray from that look, I always ended up looking overdone. It made me feel uncomfortable, and never looked pulled together. My new look is less time-consuming, and is a style that I can use even at the most formal occasion."

Shandra, 44

BEAUTY

Have an outfit or two that you know you look good in. Make sure it both fits and flatters you—and it should be comfortable. If it's "at home" wear, try to make it an outfit that you'll want to move in all day. This will prevent you from making excuses for not exercising. You'll be able to just go right out and do it. If you are in the workplace, make it something that is attractive, functional, and not binding. Clothes that restrain will make you feel bad about your body no matter what your size, and cause you stress that many times will lead to overeating.

CLONE YOURSELF

When you've found a hairdo or outfit that elicits compliments or you just know you look great in, make sure you can repeat it by taking pictures from different angles. Whenever I do a TV show, I watch carefully how the makeup artists do my makeup. Even though I've been doing my face forever, and feel I'm pretty proficient doing it, I still like to see another person's perception. If I like the look, I have someone take a picture of me. Even though I think I'll remember each step, I know I'll miss something. You can do the same by visiting different cosmetic counters and availing yourself of their complimentary makeovers. Bring a camera along. If you like what you see, have the salesperson or a friend take a close up shot.

GET OUT OF THAT RUT

There's a difference between possessing timeless style and being in a beauty rut. It's easy to fall into a rut when it comes to our looks. Many of us have our routines down pat, and it feels comfortable because we've been using the same products and styles for so long. If you think you're in a rut or you realize that you've been wearing the same look for the past five or ten years, then it's time for a change. Don't do anything drastic, because that's too scary.

It's never a good idea to do a total overhaul at once. Rather than changing your entire makeup line, why not try a new lipstick or different eye shadow? Break old habits. Have something done professionally. Try a new hairstyle. Have your eyebrows professionally shaped. If you've been living in jeans, switch to khakis. Part your hair in a different way. If you've always worn matte colors, experiment with glossy. See if a "softer" look will be more flattering. If you've been told you dress conservatively, then go to a mall, and pick something out of one of those "trendy" stores. Keep it interesting, but don't become a slave to fickle fashion trends that come and go, and can look dated in a matter of months.

BECOME MEMORABLE

It's important to have a signature look so that you will be remembered as someone who is unique. So many women will keep trying, but never capture a look that falls away from the pack. Sometimes a look is imposed upon us in school with peer pressure, or in childhood by family culture or rules. More often, it's the tired game of "playing it safe."

"Everyone remembers me as 'the girl in red.' I've loved the color red since I was a small child, *and although I don't wear red from head to toe, I'll usually be seen carrying a red purse or just my basic black dress with red pumps."*
Maggie, 41

BECOME FEARLESS

A playful style can boost your confidence. Go ahead, start breaking rules. Try on an orange lipstick. Take some beauty dares. Add some color to your wardrobe. Don't be afraid to stand out, and don't be afraid to make a mistake. Experiment until you find the look you're after. Your face is a canvas. Use foundation to even out and correct imperfections. Try new colors and combine colors you already have. Play up one feature, and you'll never look overdone. If you don't like what you've done, no problem, take it off and start again. Master two looks—daytime and evening—that you can do quickly.

MAKE THOSE FIRST SECONDS COUNT

Since the first impression is the one that remains, make it count. Ten different opinions are formed in the first minute you meet someone, including everything from financial stature to character. Think of the total picture, but don't forget the details.

Chapter 2

SUPER SKIN

FIX YOUR SKIN

Want to start looking better quickly? Fix your skin. But to be sure you're using the right treatments, you need to know what type of skin you have. Most of us begin life with normal skin. Through the years, the environment, what we eat and drink, hormones, and other factors contribute to changes and challenges. There are three types of skin: dry, oily, and combination.

DRY

Dry skin has a fine texture with small pores. It often feels "tight," and is prone to broken capillaries. Dry skin should be kept away from weather extremes, especially harsh winds.

Don't bother with soap. In the morning, dry skin only needs a splash of water to remove excess oils. Don't use any toners containing alcohol. Witch hazel is the perfect toner for dry skin. Always follow up with a rich moisturizer. Use a mild cold cream at night to remove makeup and to cleanse.

OILY

With oily skin, the pores of the skin are large and visible. The oil is especially prominent on the nose, forehead, and chin. It is prone to blemishes and blackheads. Although it seems logical to get at these eruptions with aggressive products, this makes oily skin even worse. There is not a better cleanser than powdered milk mixed with water. It is a lactic acid wash that will not only cleanse the skin, but also exfoliate debris. Lemons are a great toner to keep on hand to restore the pH balance. Finish with an oil-free moisturizer.

Although it may not seem necessary to use moisturizer at all if you're skin is extremely oily, you should always moisturize under your eyes. Use an eye gel, not a cream.

COMBINATION

This is actually two skin types on one face. Skin is usually oily only in the T zone of the face (nose, forehead, and chin) while dry elsewhere. Don't be overly aggressive with the oily area and neglect the dry spots. Use powdered milk to wash and exfoliate, use lemon toner only in the T zone, then concentrate moisturizing to the dry zones.

ACNE PREVENTION

It's not only for teens. More and more cases of adult acne have been "popping up!" Stress, which causes hormonal imbalances, is a major culprit. There are many simple ways to deal with existing outbreaks, and to prevent future ones.

• Don't try to scrub away the acne. It just causes flare ups.

• Don't try to use the sun as a cure. Although it may suppress it temporarily, it speeds up cell turnover, clogs pores, and causes skin to erupt. Always wear sunscreen.

• Be careful where you put your face. Pressing your chin against the phone, resting your hand on your cheek, or touching your face frequently can trigger acne.

• Don't use too many ingredients at one time. If you're prone to using a heavy sunscreen, rich moisturizer, and creamy foundation at one time, the combination will plug up pores.

• Hair products can be contributing factors to breakouts around the hairline, neck, shoulders, and back. Try using different products and be careful to keep them off your skin.

ACNE SOLUTIONS

• Dab garlic juice on emerging and mature pimples.

• Treat acne with benzoyl peroxide, available at pharmacies.

• Disguise a pimple with eye-redness reliever drops. Apply to Q-tip, and then hold on pimple about ten to fifteen seconds.

• Mix a packet of fast-acting yeast with enough tea tree oil to make a paste. Spread over emerging pimple, and cover with a bandage. Leave on overnight. Yeast causes the pimple to rise out of skin, while tea tree oil attacks it. It should be gone in the morning.

• Soak a cotton ball in warm salt water. Press on top of the blemish for three minutes to dissolve the top.

• Dab a bit of honey on the affected area to deep-clean the pore and draw out bacteria. Let sit for ten minutes.

SKIN REMEDIES & TREATMENTS

Take advantage of these quick and easy home remedies. Why spend time and money searching out natural, skin benefiting ingredients, when you probably have them on hand? Legendary beautiful women have always known that nothing exfoliates better than oatmeal. Forget pricey alpha hydroxy acids. You can use a paste of strawberry, lemon, or orange, anything with a low pH. Try some of the following. You'll love the superior feeling and results.

AGE SPOTS

To erase age spots, hold a lemon half directly on the age spot for ten minutes. If your arms get tired, rest your elbow on a table while applying the lemon. Rinse off with warm water.

BROWN SPOTS & DISCOLORATION LIGHTENER

Mix two tablespoons of lemon juice with one packet of raw sugar. Rub on spots with an old toothbrush. Leave on for fifteen minutes before rinsing.

BLACKHEAD REMOVER

Combine ¼ cup boiling water with one teaspoon Epsom salt and three drops of iodine. Let mixture cool until it's comfortable to the touch. Saturate a cotton ball with mixture and dab on blackheads. This will allow them to loosen so they can be easily squeezed with a gauze pad.

DRY, SENSITIVE SKIN TREATMENT

Warm ¼ cup olive oil in microwave. Make sure it's comfortable to the touch, and massage into skin. Wipe off with a cotton towel.

ENLARGED PORE TIGHTENER

Cut half of a cucumber into slices and soak in ¼ cup rose water and one teaspoon witch hazel. Refrigerate. Slide over skin after cleansing. This will reduce the appearance of the pores and tighten skin. Refrigerate the leftover solution for up to one week.

FLAKY SKIN

Massage a small amount of honey all over face. Let set about ten minutes. Remove with a cotton ball dipped in grapefruit juice. Leave on five minutes before rinsing with warm water.

HERBAL LAXATIVE STEAMER

A natural herbal laxative (available at pharmacies and health food stores) steams away impurities. There are a few, but Swiss Kriss is one of my favorites. Mix one packet with two cups of boiling water in a bowl. Put your cleansed face over the bowl (as close as you can) draping a towel over your head so that the steam will go into your face and not into the air. It is the ultimate pore cleanser. Try to relax, and stay in position for at least ten minutes. When you wipe off with your towel, you'll see debris and accumulation come right off.

INFLAMMATION-REDUCING COMPRESS

Prepare three cups of very strong chamomile tea and refrigerate in a spritzer bottle. Mist over irritated or inflamed skin.

BODY-SILKENING CUCUMBER SCRUB

Cucumbers provide gentle toning and stimulate new cell production. In a blender, mash three peeled cucumbers. While showering, apply pulp to a loofah and scrub entire body. Rinse well.

DRY, CRACKED SKIN

Mix one tablespoon dried kelp with one tablespoon vegetable shortening. Massage into dry areas. Wipe off with a coarse washcloth.

OIL-ERASING TOMATO TONER

Remove an overripe tomato's skin. In a blender, crush slightly. Using a cotton ball, apply tomato pulp to clean face. Leave on for fifteen minutes. Rinse with warm water. Tomatoes contain oil-absorbing acids and natural exfoliants.

SLEEP LINES REMOVER

If at all possible, avoid sleeping on your face. It may take some getting used to, but it will help eliminate wrinkling. If you do wake up with one of those annoying creases on your face, you don't have to face the world that way. Take a very warm, very wet, wash cloth, and hold it on the crease until it cools. Dry off the wetness with a warm hair dryer. Repeat this procedure until the crease is gone.

BODY SCRUB

Mix one cup coarse sea salt with ¾ cup peppermint tea, forming a paste. Use in the shower to exfoliate and create glowing skin.

CHAPPED SKIN

Warm cotton gloves in the dryer. Massage udder balm or petroleum jelly into chapped hands and cuticles and other chapped areas of the skin. Wear gloves overnight. Cover other chapped areas with gauze pads.

COMPLEXION RENEWER

Warm ½ cup canned coconut milk in the microwave for thirty seconds. Stir in two tablespoons honey. Massage into skin and leave on for ten minutes. Rinse with warm water. Coconut milk contains lactic acid, while honey hydrates.

SKIN LIGHTENER

Cut a lemon in half and rub it over your entire face. Let sit for about five minutes, then rinse off with warm water.

PINEAPPLE BODY POLISH

Peel one fresh pineapple and cut into four wedges. While showering, massage wedges into skin, starting at shoulders and working down to feet. Finish by cleansing with a light shower gel and rinse thoroughly.

SKIN BUFFER

Mix ½ teaspoon baby oil with enough baking soda to make a paste. Massage over skin and rinse with lukewarm water. This scrub will stimulate tired skin and leave it looking glowing.

WRINKLES

Take a vitamin C tablet (the strongest you can find), and dissolve it in ½ teaspoon boiling water. Let the water cool until comfortable to the touch. Add it to a small amount of eye cream, and pat gently under the eye and around the mouth. Vitamin C is the only topical antioxidant that has been proven to prevent oxidation of tissue.

DID YOU KNOW?

Cleopatra, whose beauty was legendary, had two cucumbers cooled daily in the River Nile for her beauty treatment. She then had them rubbed all over her body. Cucumber contains anti-wrinkling hormones and a pH of 5.5, the same as healthy skin. Use cucumbers to clean your pores and tighten skin. Rub cucumber over your legs after you've shaved or waxed them.

NATURAL SKIN SOLUTIONS

The best moisturizers and toners are no further than your grocery or health food stores. These natural products provide the results you are looking for without the chemicals and extenders that can redden and irritate the skin.

ALMOND OIL

Excellent for all skin types to soften and smooth skin. Also helpful in relieving itching, irritation, and inflammation.

ALOE VERA TONER

Apply aloe vera gel as a toner. It has healing properties to renew cells, and is very gentle to skin. Never use any toner containing alcohol. It strips the skin of natural oils.

APRICOT KERNEL OIL

Good for delicate and mature skins. Extremely rich in vitamin A.

AVOCADO OIL

Good for treating skin problems because of its high content of vitamins A and E. Use it for dehydrated or sunburned skin.

FLAXSEED OIL

High in vitamin E, and useful in promoting cell regeneration. Use it for treating stretch marks.

OLIVE OIL

Great for body and hair. Maximize the benefits by slightly warming in the microwave. Especially beneficial on very dry, cracked skin.

WHEAT GERM OIL

Excellent for sensitive skin because it can be used as both a face and eye gel. Never use a facial moisturizer on the eye area if you're prone to sensitive skin.

SKIN'S ENEMIES

SMOKING

Nicotine, tar, and smoke decrease blood flow to the skin. This causes slackness and lack of tone in the skin. It also dulls the skin's luster and creates a sallow appearance. Skin needs oxygen. It helps build collagen and elastin, and increases circulation. Exercising is better than any oxygen-enhanced cosmetic to increase the flow of oxygen to the skin. Spend thirty minutes a day taking a brisk walk rather than $30 for that oxygen-enhanced product that will produce little or no results.

ALCOHOL

Drinking too much alcohol will dehydrate the skin, expand blood vessels, and can even exacerbate Rosacea. Drink a glass of water with each glass of any alcoholic beverage to keep the body hydrated.

SUN

We all know how bad the sun is for us. Why don't you just stick your face in a frying pan? Why would you invite wrinkling to make itself at home on your face? You can get sun damage walking outdoors at noon, so always start the day with a sunscreen. I always look for a moisturizer with at least a 15 SPF protection included. This cuts down on the number of products I have to deal with, and insures its inclusion in my daily regime.

FREE RADICALS

Treat them with vitamin E capsules. Break open a 1,000 mg capsule of vitamin E with a small pair of scissors or a safety pin. Apply it directly to the skin, or mix it with a small amount of moisturizer.

EXTREME DIETING

Excessive dieting can leave your body deficient

in nutrients. This causes the body to turn to vital organs including the skin. When depleted of nutrients, skin thins, is easily damaged, and takes longer to heal. Also, constantly gaining and losing weight leaves the skin saggy and loose.

DRUGS

Some prescription drugs can cause photosensitivity. When you are given any medication, especially an antibiotic, ask about the side effects. You may need to stay out of the sun during your course of treatment.

THE TELEPHONE

The telephone is an enemy of the skin? If you've been breaking out around your chin, it probably is your telephone receiver. It's a breeding ground for bacteria. Wipe down the mouthpiece with alcohol every day. Break the habit of holding the receiver against your chin.

FACIAL EXERCISES

Although it seems to make sense that since exercise is beneficial for the body, it would similarly firm the face, it can actually accelerate wrinkling. When you exercise a muscle, the skin over it becomes wrinkled, perpendicular to the muscle action itself. The muscle goes one way, and the skin wrinkles in the other direction.

VITAMIN A

It seems odd that taking too much of a vitamin would affect the skin in a negative way. However, if you're drinking more than 16 ounces of a vitamin A fruit or vegetable juice each day, it will cause your skin to turn flakier, thinner, and give it a yellow cast.

ICE CUBES

You've heard all about how Joan Crawford and other stars boosted their skin's circulation by sticking their face in ice cubes. Don't do that—you'll end up with a face of broken capillaries.

BABY YOUR SKIN, BABY

Models have known for years that products intended for babies are gentle, effective, and save money.

BABY WIPES are great makeup removers, especially around the delicate eye area. They are also effective hand and face refreshers.

BABY MOISTURIZERS are great for all skin types, but the heavier ones are perfect for drier skin.

MOST BABY LOTIONS are double-action products that gently cleanse and moisturize at the same time. If you have a tendency to over-cleanse, these products are perfect because they won't strip skin of its natural oils. Plus, they are inexpensively priced at drugstores and mass merchandise stores.

SUNSCREEN formulated for babies contains a very high SPF. Plus, several contain balms that both cool and calm heat-irritated skin.

BABY FORMULATED SHAMPOOS are extremely gentle to hair and won't strip color.

BABY OILS AND BATH TREATMENTS contain natural, nourishing ingredients for skin. Look for brands listing lavender and chamomile as ingredients.

SPECIAL TIPS FOR LIPS

Lips need special care. Keep your pucker-uppers in top form, because not only do chapped lips look terrible, but they're prone to infections.

EXFOLIATE

Apply udder balm or petroleum jelly on your lips, and gently rub with a soft toothbrush. Apply lip balm or lipstick. This not only makes lips feel smooth, but creates that popular pouty look you've seen and admired on models.

NIGHTLY

Break open a vitamin E capsule and rub over lips. This will allow the lips to heal. In the morning, brush away the excess vitamin E. Dead skin will also be sloughed off.

LIP TREATMENT

Black tea is high in tannic acid, which boosts skin's moisture level. Saturate a black tea bag with very warm water. Press over clean lips for five minutes.

LIP PRODUCTS

Look for lip ointments containing lanolin. Look for all lip products to contain SPF protection. Another plus are lipsticks and glosses with alpha hydroxy acids. The benefits are twofold. The acids will exfoliate dead skin while they help to retain moisture.

SKIN CARE INGREDIENTS & TERMS

Reading labels is essential to buying the right skin care product, and also is helpful in comparing drug-store lines with pricey cosmetic counter skin care. Here is a brief explanation of some of the terms you should know to make an informed decision.

ASCORBYL PALMITATE:
a form of vitamin C believed to reduce wrinkles by stimulating collagen synthesis.

CERAMIDES:
synthetic replicas of lipids (moisture molecules) that form naturally in the skin. They are used in moisturizers and cleansers.

DAE:
an antioxidant compound that boosts neuro-transmitters in the skin to tighten and smooth it.

EMOLLIENT:
traps water and holds it to skin.

EXFOLIANT:
sloughs off dead, flaking skin cells that prevent moisture from penetrating skin. Reveals newer skin.

GLYCERIN:
a humectant that acts like a sponge to draw moisture from the environment.

HUMECTANT:
attracts water from air into skin.

HYDROCORTISONE:
calms redness and acne flare-ups. It also is a strong antiseptic.

ISOPROPYL ALCOHOL:
used to dissolve colorants or other ingredients into lotions.

PARA-AMINOBENZOIC ACID (PABA):
used in tanning lotions, sun blocks, and foundations.

PETROLATUM (PETROLEUM JELLY):
seals moisture into skin with a protective film. Used in cold creams and cosmetics.

POLYSORBATES:
keeps oil and water from separating. Found in lotions, deodorants, and baby products.

PROPYLENE GLYCOL:
helps retain skin's moisture (a humectant).

SORBITOL:
smoothes skin and prevents moisture loss.

STEARIC ACID:
a fatty acid that acts as a humectant when combined with glycerin.

SUNFLOWER SEED OIL:
locks moisture into skin.

TRIETHANOLAMINE STEARATE:
emulsifies oil and water in cleansing creams.

RESPECT YOUR NECK!

It's an extension of your face, and shows the first signs of aging.

SKIN PROBLEMS AND SOLUTIONS

WHITE BUMPS

These are tiny oil-filled cysts just under the upper layer of the skin. They're usually found just under the eyes and upper cheek area. Eyeglasses and sunglasses can be the culprit because sweat builds up under the frames. If that's the case, from time to time, wipe down the frames with dish washing detergent.

Also check what you're using for eye cream. An oil-free eye cream may resolve the problem.

CROW'S FEET

The skin around the eyes is the thinnest and most sensitive. Break open a vitamin E capsule and add it to moisturizer (about the amount of a thimble). Pat it under the eye in a tapping manner. Never pull or rub this delicate area.

ITCHY, FLAKY BODY SKIN

Add oils to your bath, if possible. After bathing, pat yourself dry and put on a rich body cream while the skin is still damp and absorbent.

SCARRING AND SCRAPES

Innocent scrapes, less than careful leg shaving, etc., can leave unwanted scars. Help keep skin looking beautiful by applying Neosporin immediately to new scrapes. The topical antibiotic, long known for its infection protection has been shown in clinical study to actually minimize the appearance of scars while also preventing infection.

PAPER CUTS

Dab on some petroleum jelly to ease the sting.

PUFFY EYES

• Take a metal spoon and run it under cold water. Place the metal on the puffy area for at least sixty seconds.

• Apply hemorrhoid cream (look for brands that contain ingredients of yeast and shark's liver oil) to the puffy area. Insiders have known for years that in just the way it gets the swelling out of that other area, it works the same way for the face.

• Thin cucumber slices used as compresses over closed eyes will relieve sore, puffy eyes.

• A black tea bag soaked in cold water on each eye for ten minutes will reduce swelling caused by fluid retention. Gently press from inner to outer corners to hasten drainage.

• Avoid salty foods, which cause the under eye area (and the rest of your body) to hold fluid.

• Elevate your head when you sleep to keep fluid from settling around your eyes.

DARK CIRCLES

Raw potato slices contain potassium to effectively treat dark circles. Lay down and apply the potato slices under the eye. Allow juices to absorb into the affected area.

Inexpensive, not herbal, tea bags contain tannic acid to combat dark circles. Place tea bags—with the tea inside—under the eye. Squeeze slightly so the tea doesn't run down your face. Make sure the tea bags are cool to the touch. Too warm, and they'll puff up the eye.

Soak cotton pads in rose water and apply to eye area for ten minutes.

SUN DAMAGE

Hydroquinone lightens dark freckles caused by too much sun. Test a small patch on your forearm for a day or two to make sure it doesn't irritate your skin.

INFLAMED SKIN

Milk compresses are an easy way to soothe inflamed or irritated skin. Simply soak a gauze pad in whole milk and apply to the affected area.

ROSACEA

Have you ever had a flush that lasted too long? A constant redness in the center of the face that won't go away? Although it may appear to be acne, it's probably rosacea, a skin disease that causes redness and swelling on the face.

Avoid these triggers:

Hot drinks

Spicy foods

Sun exposure

Temperature extremes

Rubbing the face

Treat with:

Aloe vera gel

Metro gel (by prescription)

Dandruff shampoo has also been found to be effective. Apply it directly. Don't dilute it.

One tablespoon dried basil leaves mixed with ¼ cup vegetable oil

ECZEMA

Itchy, red, oily patches that crop up on the backs of knees, insides of wrists, and in armpits. Treat with oatmeal baths and over-the-counter cortisone creams.

PSORIASIS

Red, raised patches with white, scaly lesions appearing on knees, elbows, hands, and scalp. A coal tar ointment is the usual recommendation, but vegetable shortening is successfully used by many, including some hospitals.

POST-WORKOUT BREAKOUTS

Moisturizer and makeup block sweat glands and clog pores, so it's important to exercise with a clean face. Very often, breakouts occur on the chest or back, caused by a heat rash. Eliminate this by avoiding synthetic materials like nylon or Lycra, which can trap moisture. Switch to breathable cotton blends, and be sure to shower immediately after your workout, using an antibacterial soap.

ITCHY, RED SKIN

Mix together:

1 teaspoon ground almonds

½ teaspoon ground orange peel

½ teaspoon powdered milk

three drops rose water

Mixture should have the consistency of a grainy paste. Gently massage into skin. Rinse with cool water.

BROKEN CAPILLARIES

Wear a sunscreen with a high SPF, and cut down on alcohol, citrus fruits, temperature extremes, and spicy foods. Treat broken capillaries with vitamin A capsules. Break one open with a safety pin and massage it in.

PERSPIRATION

Choose ingredients carefully. Products containing zirconium aluminum are more effective than those containing aluminum chloride.

ENLARGED PORES

Alpha hydroxy acids unclog pores and control oil. Mix a packet of raw sugar with enough lemon to create a spreadable consistency. Rub into nose and chin area, where large pores tend to settle. Rinse with warm water. Raw sugar is a natural glycolic acid that loosens dirt and dead skin. Pore-cleaning strips temporarily make pores appear smaller, but are not a treatment.

VARICOSE VEINS

Witch hazel has been used as a treatment for varicose veins for centuries. Available at drugstores, it should be applied straight from the bottle into the affected area. Witch hazel contains tannins and astringents which help reduce the veins by temporarily constricting blood vessels and making them less visible.

Vitamin treatments

1. Vitamin K has been proven to be highly effective in treating spider veins. Start taking it internally, and if you can find a gel cap (try health food stores), break it open and apply it directly to the vein. Tablets can be dissolved in ¼ teaspoon boiling water and either applied directly or added to any moisturizer. Be sure to massage it thoroughly into the area.

2. Horsetail extract is the No. 1 ingredient in pricey vein treatments. The generic brand is now readily available at most drug and health food stores.

BURNS

Soak the burn in milk for fifteen minutes. The fattier the milk, the more effective it will be. The fat forms a natural emollient covering on the skin. Milk works better than water because water pulls excess moisture out of the skin, and treating a burn with water requires the additional application of an emollient. For a large area, soak gauze or cloth in milk.

FRECKLES

Keep them from getting worse and prevent new ones by using sunscreen wherever your skin is exposed. To fade existing freckles, apply a mixture of boric acid powder (available at drugstores in the first aid aisle) mixed with lemon. Massage into freckled area, then rinse. Follow up with an application of hydroquinone. For very sensitive skin, mix the boric acid powder with water.

Another remedy is Retin-A, available by perscription from a dermatologist. This should be applied only at night and should fade freckles within two months.

TIRED SKIN

Bad circulation can make you look and feel tired. How many times have you awakened and not felt fully alive until you've put on your makeup? Boost your circulation and your face will glow!

Give your face a gentle massage with moisturizer. Apply light pressure in a circular motion with your fingertips. Tap your fingers all over your face as if you were playing a concerto on the piano.

CHAFING

Apply corn starch directly from the box to friction points. Cornstarch is an anti-chafing, moisture-absorbing powder.

SKIN CARE QUESTIONS

Can I use my toner all over my face?

Toner should be concentrated around the nose and chin area, and never used around the eyes. If you want to remove any traces of eye makeup, use plain water.

What is the right way to apply moisturizer?

Although you've probably heard that the only way to prevent sagging of the skin is to apply moisturizer to the face and neck in an upward motion, this is pure myth. As long as you use a light touch, the direction of the strokes is irrelevant.

What is the correct order to applying skin products?

The rule when layering is to first apply liquids, then gels, and finally lotions and creams. Always apply acne and other treatment products before moisturizers, as moisturizers form a barrier and prevent these products from getting into the skin.

What is the correct temperature to rinse off cleanser?

Slightly cool water is best. Very hot water can irritate and rob the skin of whatever protective moisture it has, while very cold water may not remove all the cleanser. Rinsing is important because cleanser only lifts the dirt from the skin; rinsing is what removes it.

What kind of soap should be used for bathing or showering?

Keep two soaps on hand for bathing. Although deodorant soap is great for certain parts of the body (armpits, groin, and feet), it is too strong for body parts that don't produce odor. For those areas (arms, legs, torso) use a milder cleanser.

No matter what I do to keep my skin soft, I can't seem to take the roughness out of my elbows.

Unfortunately, elbows have less cushioning than other body parts. Try this treatment: Mash one scoop of ripe papaya with ½ cup cornmeal. Replace in scooped out papaya and place elbow in it for ten minutes. Then, brush mixture in with an old toothbrush. Papaya's natural enzymes will loosen the dead skin cells, and the cornmeal will slough them off.

Chapter 3

HAND &
NAIL HELP

HANDS & NAILS

They're the most visible part of you, but they also take a lot of abuse. You use them in every daily activity, and yet, they are the ultimate accessory. You must give them the same attention you give your face.

BE KIND TO YOUR HANDS

What good is that $40 manicure if your hands aren't in great condition?

Rule #1
Dry your hands thoroughly after contact with water.

Rule #2
Wear gloves whenever hands encounter abuse.

Rule #3
Exfoliate and moisturize daily.

Rule #4
Avoid temperature extremes.

Rule #5
Flex and massage your fingers every day.

QUICK HAND TREATMENTS

Soften your hands even while you do the dishes. Add a little almond oil (about a teaspoon) to dishwater. The water will soften rough skin while the oil seals in moisture.

Slough off dead skin cells with a solution made of sea salt and lemon. Brush it into hands with an old toothbrush. Do this twice a week to soften hands and remove discoloration.

Wash hands thoroughly with warm water, then, using a coarse washcloth, rub briskly. While skin is slightly damp, apply a mixture of one teaspoon honey and one teaspoon olive oil. Place hands in small plastic bags, then in a pair of cotton gloves for thirty minutes. The heat helps the treatment penetrate.

GOT MILK?

Warm a cup of whole milk in the microwave for thirty seconds (or until warm, but comfortable to the touch). Soak your hands for five minutes to strengthen nails and hydrate skin. Not only is milk loaded with lactic acid, a natural alpha-hydroxy acid that gently exfoliates dead skin, but its high calcium content will strengthen fragile nails.

CUTICLE THERAPY

Soak cuticles in a solution of strong chamomile tea. Chamomile calms irritated skin, soothes away irritation, and eases redness.

Clean ragged cuticles by mixing two teaspoons pineapple juice, one egg yolk, and ½ teaspoon apple cider vinegar. Soak nails for twenty minutes before pushing back cuticles with an orange stick.

Rub equal parts odorless castor oil and white iodine into your cuticles nightly.

CUTICLE DON'TS

#1 Don't use cuticle remover. It's too harsh!

#2 Never cut cuticles. You'll risk infection.

SPEEDY FIVE-STEP MANICURE

1. Use acetone-based remover to remove old polish. If nails are discolored or stained, dab each nail with a cotton ball dipped in hydrogen peroxide. Let sit three minutes, then wipe off.

HINT: Household bleach can be used in place of hydrogen peroxide to whiten.

2. Massage olive oil into nail and cuticles. Wipe off excess with a towel.

HINT: To make your manicure last longer, dip a cotton ball in astringent, apply to nail, and let dry.

3. File tips straight across and gently round edges. Buff nail surfaces for twenty seconds each to help polish stick to nail.

4. Apply a layer of base coat or primer and allow to dry.

5. Brush on a one-coat polish containing both color and top coat.

NAIL BITING CURE

Add Tabasco sauce to your top coat. It's a spicy reminder to stop biting.

NEVER LEAVE NAIL POLISH OUT IN THE COLD

Never store nail polish in the refrigerator. This won't make polish last any longer, and may dry it out.

PROBLEMS/SOLUTIONS

NAIL POLISH BUBBLES

To keep polish from bubbling up on nails, don't shake it. Turn bottle upside down and roll gently between hands.

NAIL BREAKAGE

Avoid nail products containing formaldehyde. Instead, look for ingredients containing:

Protein: bonds and holds layer of the nail together to prevent peeling.

Calcium: helps build layers on very thin nails.

Kvlar fiber: acts as a tough shield on nails (this is the ingredient used in bullet proof vests).

Teflon: protects nails from water and chemicals by acting as a barrier.

WEAK NAILS

Buffing the nail is the secret of top manicurists for building nail strength. The massaging action not only smoothes and shines nails, it also strengthens them by increasing blood flow to the matrix, where nail growth begins.

WHITE SPOTS ON NAILS

Add zinc to your diet with zinc supplements or zinc-rich foods like eggs, milk, and liver.

NAIL FUNGUS

Thickened, discolored nails sometimes indicate the presence of a fungus. The recommended treatment is to look for anti-fungal products containing benzalkonium chloride.

CHIPPED POLISH

Any polish will chip more easily when nails are dry and brittle. This is because they lack flexibility. Massage olive oil over nail polish daily.

HINT: **To repair a chipped nail, use a file to even out edges and apply polish only to chipped area. Allow to dry, and re-coat entire nail.**

PEELING NAILS

This is usually the result of frequent exposure to harsh chemicals and detergents. Stop using acetone polish removers and other culprits. Moisturize daily with vitamin E oil or capsule.

HINT: **Try to avoid using your nails as tools, and don't give in to the temptation to pick off your nail polish. When you pick off your polish, you also might pull off the top layer of the nail.**

ROUGH PITTED NAILS

If chronic, this condition may be psoriasis. Over-the-counter cortisone creams should be used to treat the area, and adding more omega-3 fatty acids (found in fish) will prevent future outbreaks.

BRITTLE NAILS

Use lip balm or udder balm to protect and seal in moisture. Lip balm also has protective sunscreen.

HINT: **Lip balm also works to repair cracked fingertips.**

NAILS THAT WON'T GROW

Mix one packet unflavored gelatin with one tablespoon petroleum jelly. Store in an airtight container (don't refrigerate). Massage into nails daily to help them grow long and strong.

SMUDGED POLISH

Apply a bit of nail polish remover with the pad of your finger to smooth out. If necessary, add a bit of polish after it dries.

SECRET SPA TREATMENT

Every week, massage garlic oil into the nail bed and cuticle. Insiders swear that this will bring about an immediate improvement in nail length and strength. Wear cotton gloves (not only to keep the oil contained, but to keep from smelling it) and keep the oil on for at least fifteen minutes.

Wash and rinse hands thoroughly. Rub lemon on the hands to get rid of any remaining odor.

DISCOLORED NAILS
Wet a cotton swab with vinegar and press it to the nail for sixty seconds.

Chapter 4

FABULOUS FEET

PUT YOUR BEST FOOT FORWARD

Taking care of your feet is more than cosmetic. We make demands on our feet that we don't oblige on any other part of our body. Whether we're cramming them into pointy three-inch stiletto heels or walking an average of eight thousand steps a day, our feet stand up to tremendous abuse and neglect. With minimum time and effort, you can put spring back into your step.

FOOT FACTS

According to the American Orthopedic Foot and Ankle Society, 90 percent of women wear shoes that are one to two sizes too small.

Our feet don't produce any oil to prevent dry skin.

With each step, we put pressure on our feet that's up to three times our weight.

During the day, the average temperature inside a non-ventilated shoe soars to 106 degrees Fahrenheit.

THE PERFECT PEDICURE
Supplies:

Quart of whole milk

Foot basin

Orange stick

Foot file

Tissue

Base coat, polish, and top coat

1. Heat up milk to a warm, yet comfortable temperature.

2. Submerge both feet for approximately fifteen minutes.

3. While feet are slightly damp, buff hard, calloused skin with file.

4. Separate toes with tissue.

5. Push back cuticles with orange stick.

6. File down nails.

7. Apply base coat and allow to dry one minute.

8. Apply two coats of polish and the top coat.

OVERNIGHT FOOT TREATMENT

Massage petroleum jelly all over feet, concentrating on rough parts. Wear gym socks to bed. When you wake up, your feet will feel incredibly soft.

BLISTER PREVENTION

Rub petroleum jelly on every part of your feet that rub against the insides of your shoes. This will cut friction and prevent painful blisters from developing. As a bonus, your hose will be less likely to run.

FOOT RELAXERS

These relaxing rituals will relax and restore your feet as well as relieve tension.

• Apply lotion to feet and ankles with long, even strokes. Grab one foot in your hands and use thumbs to apply gentle pressure to the tops of toes, the top of the foot, and ankle. Work your thumbs in a circular motion, first clockwise, then counterclockwise. Knead the heel and ball of your foot more aggressively. Repeat with the other foot.

• Practice picking up small objects like marbles or tiny balls with your toes. Curl toes under, and hold the position to the count of ten. Repeat several times.

• Roll your foot over a cold one-liter soda bottle.

• Spread out the toes of your right foot and interlace the fingers of your left hand between them. Repeat on the left foot.

FOOT EXERCISES

BIG TOE PULL

Place a thick rubber band around both big toes and pull them away from each other. Hold for five seconds and repeat five times. This will relieve foot cramping, often the result of tight, pointed shoes.

GOLF BALL ROLL

Roll a golf ball under the ball of your foot for two minutes. Use this exercise if you suffer from foot cramps, heel pain, or arch strain.

FOOT ENERGIZERS

Fill a foot bath with very warm water. Add three drops of tea tree oil and three drops of peppermint flavoring. Soak feet for about fifteen minutes, or until water cools. Dry briskly with a coarse towel.

Mix ½ cup sea salt, ¼ cup pineapple juice, and ¼ cup aloe vera gel.

Scrub over clean feet with a stiff brush. Rinse well.

HINT: If you can't find a foot brush, use an SOS or Brillo pad.

FOOT DEODORIZERS

Add three capfuls of an antiseptic mouthwash to a foot bath. Soak feet for ten minutes. After drying, apply antiperspirant to the sole of feet.

Add ½ cup vinegar to a foot basin of very warm water. Soak until water cools down (at least ten minutes).

ODOR-ELIMINATING FOOT POWDER RECIPE

Mix together one tablespoon ginger with one tablespoon cornstarch in a small bowl.

Dust over clean, dry feet with a large blush brush.

Ginger has antibacterial properties, and cornstarch has great absorbent power.

TOP SECRET SPA RECIPE

The country's most exclusive spas charge top dollar for this foot-loving paraffin wax treatment.

1. Melt four bars of paraffin wax (available at grocery and hardware stores) in the microwave oven.

2. Massage in a rich moisturizer.

3. Dip one foot into warm paraffin three times, pausing between layers to allow them to dry.

4. Wrap each foot with plastic wrap tight enough to make an airtight seal. This will help the moisturizer to penetrate.

5. Let set for twenty minutes.

6. Remove wrap and peel off wax.

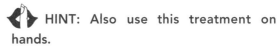 **HINT: Also use this treatment on hands.**

FOOT PROBLEMS AND SOLUTIONS

SWELLING

Besides taking off your shoes and resting tired, swollen feet, try keeping feet elevated when you sleep. Also avoid high-sodium foods, which can cause water retention.

BLISTERS

Shop for footwear made of natural fabrics. They have the ability to "breathe," where plastic and other man-made fabrics don't. It causes the shoe to "heat" and friction builds up. This increases the risk of developing blisters and other foot problems.

EXISTING BLISTERS

Apply a topical antibiotic with a cotton swab. Cover with an adhesive bandage.

INGROWN TOENAILS

Check your shoes and panty hose. Make sure that they're not too tight around the nail and surrounding tissue.

Train your nail to grow properly again. Carefully push back skin from the cuticle with an orange stick. Gently wedge a piece of cotton ball or gauze between the nail and skin.

CALLUSES AND CORNS

These occur when an area of the foot is exposed to constant pressure and friction. Prevent them by checking the pressure points of your shoes and sneakers. Get rid of them by wearing salicylic acid pads which peels away their layers. File them down with a strong emery board or pumice stone.

Chapter 5

INTIMATE INSPIRATIONS

REAL BEAUTY STARTS AT HOME!

The most important beauty routines begin before any clothing or cosmetics go on. The regimes and techniques performed in the privacy of your home are like retreating to your own personal spa. Every woman should have an area in her home that is entirely hers. It will become a welcome retreat where you can feel and look beautiful and restored, a place to take a vacation without actually taking a vacation. Try the tips in this chapter, and come up with your own favorites.

SOAK AWAY YOUR TROUBLES

Relaxing in a tub nightly for even as little as ten minutes can reduce stress and anxiety (which unfortunately shows up on your face), soothe tense muscles, and can even ease depression. Why would you miss out on this free and easy beauty enhancer?

Bath or Shower?

If possible, replace the rushed morning shower with a leisurely nightly soak in the tub. Light scented candles, put on your favorite music, and let the beauty enhancements begin.

Benefits of Bathing

• Relieve menstrual cramps with a soothing bath.

• Bathing has been known to lift depression and aid sleep.

Watch the Temperature

The water in the tub should be warm and comfortable, but not extremely hot. Water that is too hot drains energy, rather than restores it, and can dry out skin.

TUB ESSENTIALS

Have your beauty tools gathered and ready. Use a special tub basket to hold necessary supplies. ITEMS TO INCLUDE:

Bath pillow

Brush or loofah

Scents and oils

Candles

Fluffy washcloths

BATH TREATMENTS

BEFORE YOU STEP IN

Combine two teaspoons sea salt with one teaspoon vinegar. Massage on dry legs before showering.

HINT: Dry skin brushing takes only minutes and is a simple detox treatment and an effective way of stimulating the lymphatic system. It give the skin a healthy glow and breaks down cellulite.

Combine a cup of dry clay (you can use kitty litter if the label states that it is 100 percent natural clay with no chemicals or additives) and combine it with enough water to make a paste. Rub it over your body and let dry (about ten minutes). Wash off in a warm shower.

Blend one ounce jojoba oil with ½ ounce eucalyptus and ¼ ounce peppermint oil. Massage over damp legs. Cover legs with plastic wrap and leave on for fifteen minutes. Shower off.

STRESS RELIEF

Brew three cups of very strong chamomile tea. Add to bath water. Chamomile has soothing, healing properties that ease away tension.

OILY SKIN

Add to bath water any combination of citric fruits, such as lemons, oranges, and grapefruits. Citric acids kill bacteria, remove impurities, and dry up excess oil. It is the ultimate aroma therapy, and a great way to use overripe fruits.

DRY SKIN

• Add baking soda to bath water to moisturize skin.

• Fight dryness by adding ten drops of rose oil under running water. If you want true luxury, add some rose petals. Rose oil hydrates skin, is a wonderful scent, and helps prevent spider veins.

HINT: Oil and water don't always mix well. So it might be necessary to add a little milk to help them to diffuse better.

SKIN SOFTENERS

• Mix together three cups uncooked oatmeal, two cups wheat bran, and ¼ cup aloe vera gel. Spoon into a fine mesh cheesecloth or to a knee-high nylon sock. Add to bath. After soaking, use bag to cleanse skin.

• Brew ten ginseng tea bags in a large teapot. Pour into bath. Ginseng helps soften, tone, and refine skin, and it fights aging.

• Add a package of Jell-O to a warm bath. Sit in the tub for at least fifteen minutes.

SKIN EXFOLIATOR

Toss a packet of powdered milk under running bath water. Milk's lactic acid will remove dead skin cells, and leave skin's texture baby soft.

MOOD BOOSTER

• Add ¼ cup pure vanilla extract to a warm bath. Vanilla has the ability to lift spirits and revive.

• Take a handful of pine needles and place them in the foot of old panty hose. Knot around faucet, and let pine hydrate under running bath water.

ANTI-BLOATING

Mix two teaspoons ginger with two teaspoons dried mustard. Add to bath. The ingredients are perfect for menstrual bloating and discomfort.

SLEEP ENHANCER

Add two teaspoons dried lavender mixed with one teaspoon lavender oil to filled bathtub. Lavender's relaxing fragrance will put you in the mood for a night of beauty sleep.

DETOXIFIER

Add ½ pound sea salt with one pound of baking soda. Add to warm tub. Soak until water is cool.

This bath not only soothes the skin, but helps it dispose of toxic wastes.

HINT: Salt will help keep bath water warm longer. Salt slows the transfer of heat from the water to the air.

WHILE YOU'RE IN THE SHOWER

Brush your skin with a vegetable brush while showering. Use circular, upward sweeping strokes towards your heart. This method exfoliates dry skin, improves circulation, and aids elimination.

EPSOM SALTS

Keep Epsom salts on hand in the bath and shower.

• Pour a cupful in the tub to relax muscles.

• Use salts to scrub down your body in the shower to exfoliate skin and fight cellulite.

TREAT YOUR LIPS

Coat your lips with petroleum jelly. Then rub off with a wet, warm washcloth.

SOOTHE YOUR MUSCLES

Apply a thin film of bath oil over shoulders and neck. Drape a large towel over your shoulders and step into the shower. The towel's wet heat will help the oil penetrate, softening skin and relaxing muscles.

TAKE AWAY EYE PUFFINESS

Dip potato slices in yogurt and let them rest on your eyes for ten minutes.

HINT: Let face treatment masks set while you bathe. The steam speeds the penetration of nutrients into skin. Plus, the mask will work in just half the time.

BELLY BUTTON CLEAN UP

Dip a cotton swab in rubbing alcohol and wipe out lint and dirt.

FIGHT CELLULITE

Add rosemary oil to a loofah mitt when scrubbing cellulite-prone areas. It's a natural diuretic that works with steam and heat to release body of excess water, a cellulite contributor.

FEEL BETTER TO LOOK BETTER

Rub your entire scalp briskly, using your knuckles and fingertips. Grab handfuls of your hair near the roots. Gently pull your hair for ten seconds, covering your entire scalp.

Raise your shoulders as high as you can. Drop them quickly, exhaling forcefully. Repeat four or five times.

OVERNIGHT REGIMENS

The most important overnight treatment to give yourself is sleep. The skin repairs itself while we sleep, so try to get at least eight hours. Lack of sleep shows immediately on the face as puffy eyes, dark circles, bloodshot eyes, and dull-looking skin. Too little sleep can cause conditions like acne and eczema to flare up.

EYE BRIGHTENER

Combine ½ teaspoon fast-acting baker's yeast with one teaspoon whole yogurt. Stir until dissolved. Dot under eyes with a clean brush. Let dry and remain overnight. Rinse thoroughly in the morning. This solution will oxygenate the skin and diminish under-eye circles.

Place a flaxseed eye pillow over eyes (available at natural beauty shops). It keeps eyes closed while sleeping and prevents overnight puffiness.

SLEEP INDUCERS

Drizzle lavender oil on a hanky and place inside your pillow. Lavender promotes sleep-inducing alpha waves.

Adding a few drops of eucalyptus to a hanky placed inside your pillow promotes breathing. Clear nasal passages promote uninterrupted sleep.

HAND MASK

Combine one teaspoon olive oil with contents of one vitamin E capsule (1,000 units), and one teaspoon powdered milk. Massage into hands and slip on a pair of cotton gloves. Wear overnight.

FOOT SOFTENER

Warm ¼ cup petroleum jelly until it begins to melt (should still have a jelly-like consistency) with ½ teaspoon lemon juice. Massage into feet and slip on a pair of thick cotton socks. Wear overnight.

HAIR CONDITIONER

Pull hair into ponytail and adhere with old piece of panty hose. Pour one tablespoon olive oil into the palm of your hand and rub hands together. Coat ponytail until thoroughly coated. Cover ponytail with a shower cap, and wear overnight. Shampoo and condition in the morning.

SPA SECRETS

HOT STONE MASSAGE

Foot reflexology is a powerful and effective treatment. You can replicate its benefits with rocks. Hot stone massage is the latest rage at spas everywhere. Pick the smoothest rocks you can find and boil them to a very warm, yet comfortable temperature. Place them in between your toes for a few minutes, and rub them all over your feet.

HAND RELIEF

Fill a bowl with warm water, one teaspoon Epsom salt, and some playing marbles. Submerge each hand for five minutes. Roll the marbles around. It's an effortless massage and great therapy for "keyboard" fingers.

HAIR REMOVAL

THE PERFECT SHAVE

Although shaving is never any fun, taking a little extra time and effort will result in a smoother look and feel.

• Don't shave right after getting out of bed. Skin is puffy in the morning, making stubble less visible.

• Moisten hair. Hair conditioner works better than shaving cream. Soap won't hold moisture long enough, and tends to clog the razor.

HINT: To make a shave last longer, use a loofah beforehand. This helps shed the top layer of dead skin, and removes oil and perspiration for a closer shave.

• Use a fresh blade to reduce drag on your skin that can leave skin red, blotchy, and irritated. Old-time razors (the ones with replaceable blades) have heavier handles, allowing for a closer shave.

• Leave hard-to-shave spots for last. This gives these areas (backs of knees and thighs) a chance to soften.

• Start at ankles, go to bikini line, and then to underarms.

• Shave opposite hair growth. It prevents hair from curling under the skin and becoming ingrown.

• Use a light touch. To avoid nicks and cuts, exert as little pressure as possible.

• Always apply a moisturizer after shaving to prevent flaky skin.

• Bathe or shower before shaving. Hydrating hair with warm water first swells and softens stubble, producing a closer shave.

THE BIKINI AREA

The bikini area is difficult to shave because the hair grows in so many directions. Don't stop shaving this area when bathing suit season ends. Discontinuing shaving the bikini line will cause it to become overly sensitive. You don't want to have to "break" it in again.

Some women choose to trim or shave their pubic hair for hygienic purposes as well as appearance. Use cuticle scissors for safety.

HINT: A beard trimmer can be used effectively for bikini-line hairs. It leaves no unsightly red bumps. Be sure to use it at its lowest setting.

WAXING

• Avoid waxing just before or during your period. You are more sensitive to pain at this time.

• Don't shave or use depilatory at least two weeks before waxing. To be effective, your hair has to be at least ¼ inch long.

• Exfoliate between waxings to slough off dead skin which clogs pores. Use a natural bristle brush.

• Swab alcohol to ingrown hairs daily after waxing to avoid infection and red bumps.

• Before waxing, dust skin with baby powder. It helps wax adhere to hairs.

• After waxing, calm down redness with bottled or fresh lime juice.

• Apply tea tree oil (a natural antiseptic) to any raw looking areas.

• Avoid creams or lotions before you wax or the wax won't stick.

• If you're having the waxing done by a salon, try to find one that uses a natural French low-temperature wax. It will be the least painful. Ask for a wax containing azulene.

CARING FOR TEETH

It's easier than ever to have white teeth, fresh breath, and healthy gums. There have been many breakthroughs in dental research as well as new and improved products and information.

MAKE YOUR OWN TOOTHPASTE

Some of the toothpastes out there just don't do enough to whiten teeth. Others are actually dangerous and may wear off enamel and cause fillings to fall out. So, straight from the modeling world come these secret recipes that take just moments to put together.

Strawberry Toothpaste

Strawberries have gentle cleansing and bleaching properties, and help remove coffee and tea stains from the teeth. Just crush strawberry and rub the pulp directly on teeth.

Hydrogen Peroxide

Mix ½ teaspoon of hydrogen peroxide with one teaspoon baking soda. Use this tooth-whitening mixture once a week. This formula is a strong stain remover and tartar reducer. I don't recommend this treatment if your teeth are very sensitive.

FOODS THAT CLEAN TEETH

There are some foods that stain teeth (coffee, tea, red wine, etc.) and there are other foods that work on the teeth like detergents. Foods that require a lot of chewing like apples, celery, and carrots whiten teeth naturally.

Foods like spinach, lettuce, and broccoli prevent staining by creating a film on the teeth that acts as a barrier.

BRUSH YOUR TONGUE

When you are brushing your teeth, you haven't finished the job until you've brushed your tongue. Your tongue harbors germs and bacteria that can cause bad breath. Just brush your tongue with your regular toothpaste, and forget those overpriced tongue scrapers.

MAKE-IT-YOURSELF MOUTHWASHES

Tea

Boil a strong cup of peppermint or spearmint tea. Drink in a slow, deliberate manner while rolling the tea around in your mouth, or let cool and use as a regular rinse.

Clove Rinse

Heat one teaspoon of cloves with ¼ cup of water. Cool and rinse.

DENTAL CHECKUP PREPARATION

Before you visit your dentist, apply a liberal amount of lip balm to your lips. Your lips won't crack when they are stretched out.

CELLULITE

If you have cellulite, you're not alone. Over 80 percent of women have this lumpy bumpy skin. I've even worked with one hundred-pound models who have it. Although you can't cure cellulite, don't let anyone tell you there are not effective ways to diminish its appearance.

WHAT IS CELLULITE?

Cellulite is excess fat deposits, fluid, and toxins located just under the skin. It begins to form during puberty, but it's not always noticeable on younger women because their skin is more supple.

ENDERMOLOGIE

This massage and suction system is intended to improve the appearance of the bumpy and spongy appearance of cellulite. It is the only cellulite treatment approved by the FDA. Endermologie ruptures fat cells so they flatten and can't fill up again. It also stretches the strands of connective tissue that pulls skin inward and causes dimpling.

Cost: $80 to $100 per session with a commitment of fifteen sessions.

Results: Removal of up to an inch of fat from each thigh.

Note: Combining endermologie with ultrasound therapy has been found to yield even better results. Ultrasound waves liquefy fat cells from the outside before the massage begins, and can take up to 1½ pounds of fat from each thigh within the recommended fifteen sessions.

VITAMIN THERAPY

L-Carnitine and coenzyme Q 10 taken together have had some positive results. L-Carnitine pulls fat out of fat cells so they empty and flatten out, while the coenzyme Q 10 carries the fat into muscle and other body cells so it can be burned for energy. China has done extensive research in this area, and reportedly, women given 1,000 mg of L-Carnitine lost ten pounds in twelve weeks without changing their diet. Those who added 100 mg of coenzyme Q 10 lost seventeen more pounds than the first group.

BLADDER WRACK

This is one of the main ingredients in Cellasene, the newest cellulite wonder pill. It is a form of seaweed, and is high in iodine, which stimulates the thyroid, boosting the metabolism.

CAFFEINE

It's the main ingredient in most of the pricey cellulite creams on the market today. Just the way caffeine gets us going, it also gets our fat cells moving. Save yourself some money, and head to your coffee maker. Take your coffee grounds and use them as a treatment for cellulite. Some models I know ritualistically sit on the edge of their bathtubs every morning (with plenty of newspaper underneath) and rub away. This treatment works best if the coffee grounds are warm, so if they've cooled off, warm them in the microwave. Let it set for a few moments with plastic wrap around the grounds. Then brush vigorously off in the shower with a loofah.

THE HEALTHY BREAST

HOW TO WEAR THE RIGHT SIZE BRA

Eight out of ten women are wearing the wrong bra size (usually too small). This is because we don't know how to measure our breasts, and we're too modest to ask an expert. It not only affects the way our clothes look and our comfort, but wearing inadequate support can cause breasts to sag and age prematurely.

Measure your band size: While wearing a bra, pull a tape measure around your torso above the breasts and add one inch. Round up if you get an odd number like 35.

Find your cup size: With bra on, pull tape measure firmly around the fullest part of bust. Subtract band size from that number.

One inch difference = A

Up to two inches = B

Up to 3 inches = C

Up to 4 inches = D

Up to 5 inches = DD

Re-measure after pregnancy, or a weight change of ten pounds or more.

HINT: When trying on a bra, lean over to make sure breasts fit snugly and comfortably inside cups.

BREAST TREATMENT

To firm the breasts and tighten the skin, mix one teaspoon of vitamin E oil with one tablespoon of yogurt and an egg.

Massage into breasts and wear an old bra over the mixture for at least twenty minutes.

Rinse off with warm water.

FRAGRANCE FORMULAS

MAKE FRAGRANCE LAST LONGER

1. Start by layering your scent. Begin with a scented shower or bath gel. Next, apply perfumed body lotion to slightly damp skin.

2. Apply scent where skin is warmest (your "pulse" points). Use it behind the ears, on the wrist, your décolletage, and behind your knees. The heat generated in these areas will keep fragrance on longer.

HINT: Dab a little petroleum jelly onto areas where you'll spritz your perfume. This gives the scent something to adhere to.

BE AWASH IN FRAGRANCE

When hand washing fine wearables like hose and lingerie, add a few drops of perfume to the water.

SCENT STRENGTHS

Body spray	1–2 hours
Shower gel	2 hours
Cologne	3 hours
Eau de toilette	3 to 4 hours
Eau de parfum	4 hours
Body lotion	4–5 hours
Body cream	5 hours
Perfume	6 to 8 hours

SCENT YOUR HAIR

• Spray freshly washed hair with eau de parfum or cologne.

• Spray your hairbrush before brushing.

• Pour a few drops in your hands and run through your hair.

JUST A HINT OF FRAGRANCE

For those times when you want to go very lightly on fragrance, spray the air and then walk through the "cloud" in front of you.

FRAGRANCE DO'S AND DON'TS

Do wear more perfume if you have dry skin. Scent needs oils to last.

Do wear stronger scents in cold weather. Cold reduces a scent's strength.

Do wait ten minutes before deciding to purchase a new scent.

Do purchase a new scent late in the day. Your sense of smell is sharper.

Do try scents on your own skin. Everyone's skin chemistry is different.

Do choose fragrance that complements your natural body odor.

Do apply perfume right after you shower or bathe. Your pores will be open and soak up the scent.

Don't use deodorant soap where perfume is applied.

Don't use perfume near pearl or costume jewelry. The alcohol in perfumes can cause pearls to yellow and can strip the coating off jewelry.

Don't sample more than two to three new scents. Your olfactory senses will become confused.

Don't stick to one fragrance all year long. Temperatures affect the intensity of fragrance.

IN THE HOME

Spray fragrance on light bulbs. The heat from the bulb will fill the room with scent. Add a few drops of perfume to a cup of boiling water to scent your home and remove unpleasant cooking odors.

FULL BODY EXPOSURE

Whether your body will be on display for intimacy, peeling off to head to the beach, or any other body encounter of the up close and personal variety, the following tips will eliminate the most intimate body angst.

PLAN AHEAD

Pluck, wax, and exfoliate at least two days in advance to give redness a chance to go away.

ANTI-INTIMACY FOODS

Avoid gas-producing foods, especially beans and cabbage, at least twenty-four hours before that rendezvous. They can take that long to go through your system.

Other foods to avoid: Carbonated beverages, raw vegetables, onions, garlic, and curry.

BETTER BREATH

The breath mints and washes now available have become more powerful and longer lasting. Look for products containing copper or copper compounds, Retsyn, or zinc. They neutralize the sulfur that produces bad breath and last up to thirty minutes. For a longer lasting effect, choose drops containing chlorine dioxide, thymol, and eucalyptus. They fight bad breath internally.

HINT: When you're in a pinch, eat parsley. It's rich in chlorophyll, the leading ingredient in such breath fresheners as Clorets and Certs. It comes in handy when you're dining out and have forgotten your breath mints.

ACCENTUATE THE POSITIVE

Show off what you want seen, and the eyes will go there, passing over your less-than-perfect attributes. If you've got great shoulders and a drooping rear view, wear something off the shoulder. Great legs? Put on those heels and start strutting your stuff.

INTIMATE BEAUTY EMERGENCIES

SHAVING RASH

To soothe shaving irritation, chill wet chamomile tea bags, and place them on the inflamed skin. Chamomile has anti-inflammatory, antibacterial, and pain-relieving properties. For large areas of irritated skin, make a compress by dipping a gauze pad into a very strong, cold cup of chamomile tea. Apply to rash or irritation.

BRUISES

Speed the healing with vitamin K or arnica, a homeopathic plant remedy for black and blue marks. Both are available in cream or tablet form.

THIGH PIMPLES

The friction of thighs rubbing together, tight pants, panty hose, all contribute to little red bumps which resemble a bad case of acne. Besides wearing cotton and showering right after a workout, treat these breakouts just as you would the acne on your face.

EXCESS GAS

You say you can't zip up your pants because you're experiencing premenstrual bloating or you've gone a little too zealously into that high-fiber diet? Here's what models do when a photo shoot comes up and they find themselves in this very uncomfortable position.

• Have a cup of peppermint or spearmint tea, which will relax the stomach muscles and relieve the discomfort.

• Rock in a rocking chair vigorously for twenty minutes or sit on the edge of a couch and simulate a rocking position. This will release the gas.

• Take a brisk walk.

• Drink ice water.

FOOT ODOR

When the socks come off, foot odor strikes. It's not necessary to purchase expensive drugstore products. Soak your feet in strong tea (not herbal). The tannins in tea will eliminate the smell.

Hint: To prevent foot odor, apply a dry antiperspirant deodorant to your soles every morning.

INGROWN HAIRS

Ingrown hairs are usually a result of shaving, and women with curly or course hair are particulaly susceptible to them.

• Stop ingrown hairs before they start by shaving over each area only once.

• Change blades regularly to prevent bacteria from building up and contributing to infection.

• Shave slowly and carefully, pulling skin taut as you go.

• Use an abrasive pad in a warm shower to open pores.

WARTS

I got this tip from a well-known hand model I worked with. Break open a vitamin E capsule and apply it to the area surrounding the wart. Then, crush a clove of raw garlic, place it on the wart, and cover it with an adhesive bandage. The raw garlic causes a blister to form, and the wart will fall off within a week. Keep applying vitamin E to the area to help it heal.

HEEL PAIN

This type of pain can be caused by three inch stilettos or exercise. Slowly roll your bare foot back and forth over a tennis ball. Roll for a full minute on each foot.

HANGOVER

A hangover will definitely show on your face. To keep the skin hydrated and flush out toxins, drink two liters of water. Drink it at room temperature because it will be easier to digest.

DEODORANT STAINS

If your clothing picks up deodorant stains, try dusting some baking soda under your arms instead. It absorbs perspiration and neutralizes odor. Plus it allows you to dress without having to wait for your deodorant to dry.

SUNBURN

A bottle of vinegar added to a warm bath will both soothe a sunburn and make skin feel extra soft. Try raspberry vinegar for the added touch of aromatherapy.

CUTS

Sprinkle cayenne pepper directly on the wound. It will stop the bleeding.

URINARY TRACT IRRITATION

If it's mild enough to be only irritating, stock up your fridge with blueberries and cranberry juice. Both contain large amounts of antioxidant rich anthcyanins.

If the irritation is not cleared up in a day, it could be more serious and needs to be checked by a physician. Urinary tract infections should be treated immediately.

COLD SORES

Catch the warning signs of an oncoming cold sore. A tingling sensation starts about twelve hours before the sore appears. Dab a little Pepto-Bismol on the sore. Just the way it fights the virus that causes diarrhea, it combats a cold sore.

SKIN BURNS

Place a bag of frozen vegetables on the burn (smaller vegetables like peas and corn work best). Crushed ice cubes wrapped in a thin towel also work. The ice helps to constrict blood vessels, reducing swelling and inflammation. Hold for at least fifteen minutes.

HINT: I find that if the burn is small enough (like a cooking burn on the hand), a frozen baby's teething ring works like a charm!

INTIMATE BEAUTY QUESTIONS

These embarrassing questions have more than once been passed anonymously to me when I am doing a speaking engagement and ask for questions from the audience.

Is it okay to dye pubic hair?

With proper application, hair coloring on pubic hair is no more risky than it is on the hair on your head. The good news is that pubic hair grows more slowly, so you won't have to dye it nearly as often. That said, don't color your pubic hair if you're pregnant or trying to conceive. And be careful to keep the dye only on the hair. Try not to get any on the labia.

Is it safe to use public rest rooms?

Ladies' rooms contain lots of harmful bacteria. Be careful and do the following:

• Use the first stall. It's the least used, so it's least likely to be contaminated.

• After washing hands, turn off the faucet with a paper towel.

• Air blowers are not as safe as paper towels. Blowers collect bacteria from the air and deposit them on your hands.

• Avoid setting your purse on the floor.

• If you drop something, immediately wash it with soap and water. Then disinfect it with an antibacterial gel.

• Don't touch the sanitary napkin disposal unit. It's the most contaminated area in the rest room and loaded with fecal bacteria.

Chapter 6

INSIDE/OUT BEAUTY

BEAUTY ISN'T JUST SKIN DEEP

What you eat affects your looks. There's not a question about it. Foods affect your appearance in the very same way they nourish your body. Why sabotage your health and your looks at the same time with unwise food choices? You've got to eat, so why not eat to look and feel better? When I see a woman who looks absolutely radiant, I know that she is doing more than spending lots of money on cosmetics. What we put inside of our bodies is even more important than what we put on the outside.

WATER

Keep hydrated by drinking lots of water. Hydration can definitely improve the skin. Water regulates our body temperature, removes waste, protects our organs, helps convert food to energy, and cushions our joints. Too little water causes the skin to become dry and flaky. Water also can help you diet. Water cleanses the system while filling you up. Flushing the system of toxins helps to keep skin glowing and weight under control. Plus, the more you drink, the less your body will retain extra fluid. Try to drink at least eight glasses of water a day.

HINT: The body burns up to twenty-five calories just by turning up its metabolism in order to warm a glass of water.

THE BEAUTY FOODS

Apple Cider Vinegar

Besides having amazing healing properties, apple cider vinegar keeps skin supple. Its heavy concentration of enzymes helps peel off dead skin cells. It breaks down fat and helps food digest properly.

Carrots

Maintain the outer layer of the skin to prevent premature aging. What you'll find in carrots is the same as you'll get in Retin A.

Cheese

To ensure a happy smile, add a slice or two of hard cheese into your diet. Choose Swiss, cheddar, or gouda to block bacteria in the mouth and prevent cavities.

Citrus Fruits

Hold the skin cells together by forming collagen. Collagen cannot be added to the skin topically, which is why fruits and fruit juices are such an important part of the daily diet.

Cranberries

Keep the urinary tract lining healthy.

Garlic

Helps combat wrinkles and restores tissue.

Nonfat Yogurt

High in calcium, which keeps your smile white and your teeth cavity-free.

Sweet Potatoes

Vitamin A is known to be a remarkable anti-wrinkling agent. Sweet potatoes are full of this important vitamin. The pleasing result is clearer, smoother skin.

Tomatoes

These "love apples" will keep you loving your skin. Tomatoes are rich in vitamin A, vitamin C, and potassium.

Wheat Germ

If you want to get rid of pimples quickly and efficiently, make sure to include two or three tablespoons a day in your diet. Add it to cereal, yogurt, and cottage cheese.

WHAT TO EAT EACH DAY FOR LOOKS AND HEALTH

You should choose foods that you enjoy, of course, but you need to include the following:

Vegetables

Three to five servings daily.
Try to include one serving of raw, leafy greens.

Meat

Have no more than three three ounce servings a day.
Cut off all fat.
Try to make two servings turkey or chicken.
One serving of fish a day is ideal.

Fruits

Two to three servings daily.
A ½ cup of chopped or sliced fruit is a serving.

Dairy

At least two servings daily.
A serving would be eight ounces of milk or yogurt.
1½ ounces of cheese is a serving.

Fats

Salad dressing, cooking oil, butter, and mayonnaise should be limited to two servings a day.

ENJOY THAT COFFEE BREAK

Fresh-brewed coffee contains cancer-fighting antioxidants that are just as strong as vitamins C and E.

TAKE A BITE OUT OF YOUR BEAUTY PROBLEMS

If you've been suffering from ongoing beauty problems, look to the foods you've been eating. You'll be amazed at how quickly small changes in your diet can solve each and every one of them. Be patient, these changes won't happen overnight.

WRINKLES

Add leafy green vegetables and fresh fruits like peaches and apricots. These foods are rich in vitamin A, which prevent aging and repairs the outer layer of the skin.

BLOATING

Whether it's puffy eyes or general bloating, cutting down on sodium will produce immediate results. Try to stay away from carbonated beverages, even diet soda. Stay away from processed foods like canned soups, crackers, and chips. Replace salt with herbs and spices to flavor your foods. If you do enjoy the occasional diet soda, drink a glass of water with it to diffuse some of the bloating.

BRITTLE NAILS

Problems like brittle nails and hair may indicate a need for more protein. The best protein choices are meat, chicken, and fish. Non-meat eaters should add protein-rich beans.

LIFELESS HAIR

I can usually spot someone who's gone into an extreme dieting mode by the texture of her hair. It becomes dull and lifeless due to the lack of fat in the diet. Add good fats like olive oil and fish oil.

FEED YOUR HAIR

It is essential for healthy hair that you eat the right foods. Hair is largely made up of vitamin B complex and protein. Choosing foods rich in these nutrients will create a remarkable and almost immediate improvement. Concentrate on foods like red meat, carrots, broccoli, and fish. To obtain even quicker results, add vitamin B and marine protein complex supplements.

GRAY HAIR

Premature graying may be the result of diet. Trace minerals such as iron and copper maintain hair pigment. The best way to add iron to your diet is with red meat. Those of you who try to stay away from red meat should start adding eggs and dark-colored vegetables and fruits.

YELLOW SKIN

Add lemon to your diet. Spritz it on your salads, in each glass of water you drink, and on fish and vegetables.

DRY SKIN

Start drinking more water right away. It keeps skin hydrated. Add olive oil, fish oil (sardines are great if you have the palate for them), and nuts to your diet.

SKIN RASH

Remove fried and fatty foods from your diet. Stay away from sugar-laden foods, and drink more water to improve elimination. Rashes can result from toxins in the body.

PALE SKIN

Add iron to your diet by eating red meat. Vegetarians, who are prone to pale skin, should eat more spinach and broccoli.

SPIDER VEINS

Stay away from caffeine, and start drinking more water. Start each day with a cereal with at least five grams of fiber.

SUPPLEMENTING YOUR BEAUTY

There's not a woman who truly cares about her looks who doesn't supplement her diet on a daily basis. If we were to try to do this with food, we would find ourselves consuming too many calories. For looks, vitality, and well-being, supplements are playing an important role in the regimens of the world's most beautiful women, and they should be in yours. There is nothing topically that can compete with the internal treatment of the body.

HINT: When you can get combinations of the following, it certainly will make it more convenient. Check RDA recommendations.

VITAMIN A

Take this supplement to regulate skin hydration, and to repair skin and nails. Vitamin A builds bones and keeps teeth strong. It stimulates the growth of skin cells and is used to treat acne.

Important: Pregnant women should keep total consumption below 10,000 units daily. High doses has been linked to birth defects and miscarriage. Check with your doctor about a vitamin supplement plan.

VITAMIN B

This important supplement keeps skin smooth, promotes hair and nail growth, and improves circulation.

BEE POLLEN

The buzz on bee pollen is that it has anti-aging benefits while providing an extra energy lift. Health enthusiasts use it as coffee alternative.

Warning: Users have reported allergic reactions and sensitivity.

BETA CAROTENE

This vitamin A precursor protects cell membranes and skin cells from free radical attack. This means that it will help skin retain moisture.

BIOTIN

A member of the B vitamin family, it aids in cell growth. Improvements in hair growth and thin, splitting nails have been linked to biotin.

BLUE GREEN ALGAE

This hot new food supplement boosts energy levels, detoxifies the body, and heightens mental acuity. Dedicated users report that the capsules have allowed them to require less sleep and less food, and has boosted their creativity.

BORAGE OIL

This supplement is useful in treating skin disorders and contributing to skin health. It is a natural oil that not only restores moisture and smoothness to dry and damaged skin but provides treatment to scaly skin problems. Take it to improve skin texture.

VITAMIN C

This has been proven to protect the skin and to fade age spots and other pigment irregularities. Vitamin C is essential to the formation of collagen, which cements the skin cells together. Without enough of this vitamin, skin becomes bumpy and wrinkled. Vitamin C also shrinks pores by helping oil-secreting glands to properly function.

CAT'S CLAW

Known as the Peruvian wonder herb, cat's claw comes directly from the ancient rain forest of the Amazon. A natural antioxidant, one of the major benefits is that it acts as an anti-edemic (takes down swelling). Use it to relieve swollen ankles and general bloating, and for PMS symptoms.

CHOLINE

This supplement metabolizes fat and cholesterol and aids in hormone production. It is taken to delay the effects of aging.

COENZYME Q 10

Produced in the body naturally, it is being hailed as a supplement to enhance the power of the brain and prolong youth. Researchers report that mice given coenzyme Q 10 lived longer and remained extremely active. It is taken by beautiful women everywhere because it fights wrinkles from the inside.

DANG GUI

Also known as dong quai and tang kuei, here is a highly versatile supplement to include in your list. From its name, it is obvious that its origins are from ancient Chinese medicine. Usages include treatment of menstrual abnormalities (cramps, PMS) and menopausal symptoms. It also is used in treating gas and bloating.

DHEA

This supplement is short for dehydroepiandrosterone, a hormone made by the adrenal glands located just above the kidneys. Being touted as "the fountain of youth," its benefits include everything from more energy (including sexual energy), to firmer skin and thicker hair. Formerly available only by prescription, DHEA is now sold everywhere. It is recommended that 25 mg be taken starting at age thirty-five until fifty. After fifty, the dosage should be increased to 50 mg.

VITAMIN E

This one's known as the skin vitamin. It's properties have the capability to heal scar tissue and to neutralize damaging free radicals. It does this before they have a chance to appear on the skin.

ECHINACEA

Echinacea helps to activate the immune cells. Take it when you feel a virus or cold coming on,. and to treat skin problems such as boils, burns, wounds, stings, hives, insect bites, and eczema. Take it only on an "as needed" basis as it has no cumulative effect.

EVENING PRIMROSE OIL

It benefits the skin and hair, and is also taken to restore hair growth and keeping hair shiny and sleek. It is a highly effective supplement for softening dry skin.

FLAXSEED OIL

Reports indicate that flaxseed oil has helped hair to grow by increasing blood circulation in the scalp.

GLA

Gamma-lineolic acid (GLA) is legendary for creating supple, smooth skin. It does this by sealing in moisture, reversing sun damage, and helping skin to retain elasticity.

GINGKO BILOBA

It increases alertness, improves memory, and circulation. It is taken as a general anti-aging supplement.

GINSENG

This very popular supplement has many health and longevity benefits. It improves energy levels as well as enhances mental alertness. Ginseng also is reported to lower cholesterol levels and strengthen the immune system.

GRAPE SEED EXTRACT

Antioxidants in grape seeds protect the thin walls of blood vessels from losing their strength. Take it to prevent and correct the appearance of spider veins.

GROUND ANTLER TIPS

Top stars swallow ground antler tips to strengthen the body and enhance sex drive. Available in both ampules and tablet form, no animal is ever harmed. Deer antler tips are sloughed off naturally. There are farms in Canada where the deer live very comfortably and are raised only for their valuable antlers. The beauty benefit is that these tips rebuild collagen from within.

VITAMIN K

This is the No. 1 recommended supplement for the treatment of spider veins, bruising, and broken blood vessels. It also works to cure under-eye circles and blotchy red skin.

KOMBUCHA

Here is a mushroom derivative that all of Hollywood loves. It is readily available as a tea or in capsule form, and is used as a detoxifying agent. Devotees claim it dramatically improves energy levels and well-being.

MELATONIN

Known as a natural sleep aid, jet lag reducer, and mood enhancer, there is also definitive research that melatonin has some anti-aging potential. The recommended dosage is from 1 mg to 3 mg.

MSM

Everyone is talking about this hot new beauty miracle pill. MSM is an essential building block of keratin, the protein that makes nails and hair strong and healthy. Benefits include thicker hair, stronger teeth, and break-resistant nails. The recommended dosage is 750 mg daily.

PREGNENOLONE

This hormone is produced naturally in our bodies, but decreases after the age of thirty-five. Not only does it contain outstanding anti-aging benefits, but it makes it easier to lose weight and improve muscle tone. The recommended dosage is 10 mg no more than three to four times a week.

PYCNOGENOL

A compound from the French maritime pine, this powerful antioxidant acts similarly to vitamin E, but with fifty times the strength. It boasts twenty times the strength of vitamin C. It also protects the cells membranes from sun damage, provides capillary support, and helps preserve collagen. It is powerful in helping to maintain firm, young-looking skin. Pycnogenol also helps relieve PMS symptoms and breast tenderness.

ROYAL JELLY

Swathed in the mysteries of the ancient Orient, here is one of the most enduringly popular food supplements. Royal Jelly is a unique, high protein food in its raw state. It's produced by bees and fed to their offspring. Used as a food supplement, it is available in both capsule and liquid form. Purists prefer the liquid because it is more readily absorbed into the system. Use it for overall health and stamina.

HINT: Local Chinese supermarkets and Chinese neighborhoods generally have better price points on these and other supplements.

SEAWEED

What you usually avoid at the beach has great health benefits. It's sold in both dried form and in tablets. Models like to reconstitute it and add it to soups and salads. If that doesn't tempt your taste buds, purchase the tablets. The most popular are Dulse and Kelp. Take it for its rehydrating benefits and to boost a sluggish thyroid.

SELENIUM

Take this vitamin to enhance the effects of vitamin E. Selenium has a close metabolic interrelationship with vitamin E and aids in tissue growth and regeneration. Selenium's role is to keep skin elastic and youthful.

SILICA

Beauties swear by this supplement for radiant skin, luxurious hair, and rapid, strong nail growth. It also provides collagen to the body.

SPIRULINA

Used by weight-conscious beauties worldwide, spirulina is believed to dampen the appetite. It is a rich source of phenylalanine, a natural occurring substance that creates a feeling of fullness. It's readily available in most drugstores and mass merchandisers.

VANADYL SULFATE

This nutrient helps to build lean muscle tissue by increasing amino acid uptake.

ZINC

This mineral aids in wound and scar healing and is essential for the formation of collagen. Zinc helps tissue and cell growth. The recommendation is 60 mg a day.

Although the specific hour is not really important when taking supplements, doing it at the same time creates a routine. In this way, you will make this as important to your beauty regime as putting on your makeup.

WHEN TO TAKE SUPPLEMENTS?

HINT: Some supplements are better absorbed if taken with food.

THE IMPORTANCE OF ELIMINATION

When it comes to beauty it's important to consider the role of regularity. If your body is not flushing out toxins regularly, it will show on your skin, which is also responsible for releasing wastes. It can appear as breakouts, rashes, and pallid, lackluster skin. Although there have been models, actresses, and other great beauties obsessed with inside/out beauty, it should become an integral part of the total beauty regimen in everyone's lives. The legendary sex siren Mae West was known for her silky skin and her daily enemas. Colonic cleansing is the big rage in Hollywood, but it's unnecessary and expensive.

FIBER AND WATER

Fiber and water are the two most important vehicles for proper elimination and health.

There are two types of fiber to consider when reading labels.

Soluble Fiber

Lowers cholesterol.

Insoluble Fiber

Combats constipation, hemorrhoids, and colon cancer.

Water

You need lots of water to push wastes and toxins through your system. Try to drink about eight glasses daily.

FRUITS AND VEGETABLES

Detoxify the body by eating fruits and vegetables. Try to eat as many fresh foods as possible, including the skin, for optimal fiber intake.

SUPPLEMENT YOUR FOOD

FATTY ACIDS

It's important to include enough fatty acids in your diet to help the body retain moisture. Always choose unsaturated fats such as flaxseed oil, olive oil, and safflower oil.

FLAXSEED

Flaxseed is an excellent source of fiber. Some cereals have it (check labels, it will be listed), and it can be purchased at most health food stores. Keep it stored in the refrigerator.

HINT: Grind up a tablespoon in a coffee grinder or food processor. Sprinkle it on cereal or yogurt, or add crunch to your favorite salad.

POTASSIUM

Potassium-rich foods such as bananas, whole grains, leafy greens, and tomatoes help to regulate body/water balance.

BODY-DETOXIFYING FOODS

BROCCOLI

A great food, not only for looks and vitality—researchers have found that broccoli also helps to lower the risk of some cancers.

CABBAGE

Sulforophane, found in this much-maligned food, helps the liver process harmful toxins more efficiently. Other foods containing this important detoxifying ingredient are kale and brussel sprouts. Cabbage also helps the body to process harmful estrogen that's been linked to breast cancer.

OILY FISH

Especially oily fish such as mackerel and sardines will keep skin moist while combating breast cancer and heart disease.

SOY

Some of the many benefits of soy include easing symptoms of menopause and lowering rates of breast cancer. Soy milk, soy beans, and soy-based tofu are ways to add this to your diet.

• Pour soy milk on cereal.

• Substitute tofu for soft cheese in recipes.

• Use tofu as a dip with lots of seasoning.

• Substitute soy for half of the meat required in chili and sauce recipes.

• Use soy flour in recipes, but for no more than one-third the amount required. Soy flour does not contain the gluten necessary to cause baked goods to rise.

YOGURT

Another detoxifying food, it also builds strong bones and prevents osteoporosis.

CELEBRITY INSIDE BEAUTY TIPS

Rebecca Romijn-Stamos learned early in her life from a nutrition-minded mother about an inside approach to beauty. This super-driven super model is a big believer in daily supplementation, especially vitamin C.

Naomi Judd is extremely aware of a nutritional approach to beauty. This lovely singer does not take health for granted since her 1990 hepatitis C diagnosis. She credits part of her remission to a type of massage that drains the lymphatic system, as well as a diet rich in antioxidant foods such as leafy greens, broccoli, and asparagus.

Stephanie Powers is still a remarkable-looking beauty who is now in her late fifties. One of her longtime secrets is her inside/out approach to her looks. She strongly believes in wholesome foods, and takes the supplement gingko biloba. She claims it contributes to both her high energy level and her positive state of mind.

Goldie Hawn looks even better in her fifties than she did when she graced our TV screens in her pop-art dancing antics on *Laugh-In*. She often makes her own beverage concoctions with a blend of celery, kale, parsley, and peppers.

A star who believes in proper elimination is **Reba McEntire**. Three times a day, she takes the herb Black Rodist (available at health food stores and natural supermarkets). It is popular with many stars in Hollywood for its ability to detoxify both the bowel and lymphatic systems.

Christina Applegate is a big believer in soy products. She prides herself on maintaining a healthy kitchen filled with vegetables.

Josie Bisset, the former *Melrose Place* star, is a big believer in the benefits of both fiber and soy. Her day begins with oatmeal or Raisin Bran with soy milk. Dinner is a tofu-based meal for its soy content or fish for its omega-3 oils.

What is **Melanie Griffith's** "inside" secret to looking better than ever in her forties? Credit her daily dose of a soy protein shake. She starts every day with it, and you can copy her recipe. Blend one cup of berries (blueberries, strawberries, etc.), a scoop of soy powder, ¼ cup apple juice, and one cup of ice.

HINT: Most celebrities use their blenders and food processors daily. Get one that also crushes ice.

Chapter 7

QUICK FACES

YOUR BEST FACE FORWARD

There's no excuse not to do something to make yourself look better. It doesn't have to take a lot of time. A few strokes here, a dab or two there, and your face will become more attractive and interesting. With the right makeup and the proper techniques you can look prettier, younger, or just a little bit better. Your face is a canvas, and you are the artist.

START WITH A CLEAN SLATE

Always apply makeup to a fresh face. Your make-up will go on smoothly and evenly, and will last much longer.

Always apply a moisturizer after cleansing to ensure makeup will not seep into pores.

GET RID OF FACIAL HAIR

Quickest and cheapest: depilatories, waxing, and tweezing

Note: If you are using Retin-A, Accutane, or Renova, discontinue use for at least two weeks before waxing.

Longest lasting but most costly: electrolysis and laser

Note: I've worked with makeup artists who insist on shaving a model's face before applying their makeup. This is fine if it's done occasionally, using a sensitive razor. It gives an incredibly smooth appearance for close ups!

EYEBROWS

A good eyebrow will perfectly frame the face. You're missing an important beauty asset if your eyebrows are not properly groomed. A properly shaped brow makes eyes look bigger and cheekbones look higher. It gives the face strength and expression. Don't be afraid to tweeze your brows yourself. It doesn't have to hurt (well, not very much), and it doesn't take as much time as you would expect. Here's how to make it fast and easy.

Which Tweezer?

Thin Tip: Good for grasping small, fine hairs, and plucking ingrown hair.

Slanted Tip: Gives maximum control.

Square Tip: Best used for removing coarse hairs or several hairs at a time.

1. Tweeze immediately after showering or apply a hot washcloth to loosen hair follicles.

2. Hold a pencil vertically along the side of the nose. Eyebrow should start at outside edge of pencil.

HINT: Leaving a bit more space will widen close-set eyes.

3. Hold pencil to outside of eye. This is where the eyebrow should end.

4. Smooth brows with a little moisturizer to help hairs slide out.

5. Brush brows up to find a natural arch.

6. Draw in the desired shape beforehand with a soft eye shadow pencil.

HINT #1: Don't use an eyeliner pencil. It will cause you to pluck too much.

HINT #2: Don't use a magnifying mirror. You'll end up tweezing too much or tweezing each brow differently.

7. Tweeze under the brow first, plucking in the direction of the growth.

HINT #1: If plucking becomes too painful, apply a little Anbesol (yes, that pain reliever for teeth also numbs brows).

HINT #2: Try not to pluck just before your period. Your skin is more sensitive.

8. Using an eyelash comb, comb brows upwards and trim any hairs that extend beyond the natural top or brow bone.

9. After tweezing, soothe the area with cool, wet tea bags.

Eyebrow Bleaching

There a few makeup artists who are strong advocates of bleaching eyebrows to "open" the eye. Although lightening brows does lighten the face and give a softer all-over effect, be very careful if attempting this at home. You could end up with orange eyebrows. Some stylists will give you bleach, while others will do the bleaching for you.

Do-It-Yourself Bleaching

If you want to try bleaching your brows yourself, use facial hair bleach. Carefully coat the brows and keep checking the color every few moments. Don't worry about getting an exact match to your hair color.

No Time to Tweeze?

Shape them by brushing in an upward motion and holding their shape with a dab of petroleum jelly.

Eyebrow Stubble

Sometimes eyebrow hairs are too short to tweeze, yet too visible to ignore. Here are three ways to camouflage the problem:

• Use a concealer under the brow to hide the regrowth.

• Apply a soft, neutral shadow over entire eyelid to eyebrow.

• Feather the eyebrow down to blend into the ingrown hairs.

The Best Brow

To prevent eyebrows from looking too dark, unnatural, or drawn-on, follow these expert tips.

• Use small strokes along the line where you want your eyebrow placement.

• Always use a neutral color (taupe is a model's favorite) no matter what your brow color.

HINT: If you want to match your brow to your hair color, draw in first with a neutral-colored pencil, and then brush over the brow with a powder shadow and a small angled rigid brush. Wet the shadow slightly to make it more lasting.

• Find a pencil with a soft texture. It will draw in a softer, more natural line.

• Spray a toothbrush with hairspray or dip finger into petroleum jelly.

HINT: Eyebrows should shine, just like hair. It illuminates the face.

• Brush brows up and into place.

IF YOU'RE NOT SURE what brow looks best for your face, go to a professional for your first plucking.

THE ESSENTIAL TOOLS

Unless you have the right tools, all the beauty products in the world won't do you any good. You don't have to get your tools at the cosmetic counters. They are never worth their pricey tags. Most makeup artists get their brushes from art supply stores.

BASICS

Sponge applicator for all-over eye color

Small eye-shading brush to concentrate eye color

Old toothbrush to groom eyebrows

Eyeliner brush

Wedge-shaped sponges to apply foundation and concealer

Lip brush

Metal eyelash curler (if you're nervous about using one, a metal spoon works well)

Powder brush

Blusher brush (smaller than a powder brush)

HOW LONG DOES MAKEUP LAST?

There's a shelf-life to those cosmetics. Keeping cosmetics too long renders them useless. They get dry, smelly, and cause breakouts.

Liquid Foundation: One year. Signs that it's time to go: strange color, odor, and thickening.

Lipstick: One to two years. Look for odor, stickiness, and breakage.

Eye Shadow: Two to three years. The color may change and it will stop going on smoothly.

Mascara: Four to six months. It will start to dry out, clump, and have an odor.

USE YOUR HANDS

The more you can use your hands to apply your makeup, the more comfortable you'll become with your face. The result will be a more natural, blended face. Use your fingers to warm your concealer and foundation to make it easier to spread.

Professional makeup artists use their hands to do all sorts of makeup tricks. They blend different colors on the back of their hand, sometimes adding concealer or foundation to lighten a shade. Often, they will use lip balm or petroleum jelly to change texture.

THE RIGHT FOUNDATION

With so many varieties of foundations on the market today, as well as over fifty shade selections, finding the right foundation can be daunting. If your skin is oily, you will want to use an oil-free or water-based foundation. Dry skin works best with a liquid foundation or rich cream.

Test foundation just under the jaw line. This will immediately let you know if it will be invisible on the face. The mistake many women make is to test color on the cheek, which is often darker than other parts of the face, or worse, on the back of the hand.

Women of color have yellow pigment, so they should look for foundations with yellow undertones in oil-free formulations. Darker skin reflects more light and is generally more oily.

Application

1. Moisturize face and let it absorb. This keeps foundation on top of the skin.

2. Stroke it on and blend quickly.

3. Set it by dipping a brush into powder and going over the face in circular strokes. Don't worry about getting every bit of shine off your face. A matte face looks dated.

HINT: Long-wearing foundation is usually too dry to use around the eye and mouth. Add a little moisturizer to the foundation and gently pat into these areas.

Foundation Tricks

• Tap foundation on with a sponge or finger. Your skin will look luminous, yet natural.

• To give the skin a dewy finish, moisten a gauze pad or wash cloth in astringent and gently pat your already made up face. The astringent (witch hazel is perfect) will remove the matte look of makeup, while leaving the skin radiant.

• Open your mouth when applying foundation to expose the neck area and eliminate an obvious line at the jaw line.

• Keep two shades of foundation on hand. One will be suitable for winter, and the other for summer skin. Most of the year, they will match perfectly if mixed together.

• After your makeup application, take apart a tissue, and pat over your face. It blends the makeup together while softening the look.

CONCEALER

The right concealer can hide just about every imperfection and give you flawless skin. Gently pat concealer on with fingertips, or brush on with a soft flat brush. Anyone who has less-than-perfect skin needs a good concealer.

HINT: Concealer should cover entire under-eye area, including outside of eye to give it lift. The outside of the eye is also prone to redness and dryness.

What Kind?

Liquid concealer is especially recommended for dry skin and for concealing large areas like under-eye circles.

Solid concealer is necessary to hide stubborn pimples, scars, and bruises.

A more natural looking concealer is a cream-to-powder foundation. Match it to the shade of a liquid or cream foundation.

HINT: With liquid or solid foundation, best results are obtained by using concealer afterward. When using a cream-to-powder foundation, concealer should go on first.

Expert Tricks

• Add yellow eye shadow to concealer or foundation to conceal dark circles. It will color-correct dark undertones while concealing.

• Blue or green eye shadow added to concealer or foundation will correct ruddy tones and broken capillaries.

• Use the residue in the cap of your foundation as the perfect concealer. It's slightly dehydrated, making it just the right thickness to conceal. And of course, it matches your foundation beautifully!

EYES

Your eyes should be the focal point of your makeup. They are the first feature to be noticed. The general rule of color: The darker the eye, the deeper the eye product. Darker skin tends to absorb color. Use rich eye colors like gold, deep grays, violets, coppers, navy, and browns. Light-eyed beauties should select taupes, light grays, ginger, khaki, and specific blues.

HINT: **Always have white eye shadow on hand. It opens the eye when applied on the inner eye, and lifts the eye when applied at the brow bone. It also softens a harsh look resulting from a heavy hand.**

HINT: **Keep baby oil on hand to create creamy consistencies to eye shadows and blush.**

YOU NEED THREE EYE SHADOW COLORS

To achieve a simple, polished look for eyes, choose three similar shades of eye shadow.

1. Apply the lightest shade from lash line to brow.

2. Apply a medium shade from lash line to just above crease.

3. Use an eyeliner brush with a dark shadow to line around the lash line.

HINT: **To keep eye shadow from creasing, first dust the lid with powder. It creates an oil-free surface to ensure shadow goes on smoothly.**

HINT: **To achieve a long-lasting wet look on your eyelid, use a lip gloss all over the lid before applying powder. The shadow will stick to the gloss base.**

EYELINER APPLICATION

Close-Set Eyes: Line outer third of upper lids with gray, brown, or black liner. Smudge gently. Use a lighter liner on the inner eye to widen the space between eyes.

Small Eyes: Draw a dark line gradually thickening at outer edge of eye. Use a light-colored pencil (gold, silver, white) and draw under lower lash.

Deep-Set Eyes: Line upper lash line with a pale, shimmery liner. Then line outer edge of lower lash with a soft, neutral shade (gray or taupe). This will create the illusion of a less heavy lid.

Drooping Eyes: Line outer third of eye very close to lashes, carefully sweeping the liner up at the corner of the eye.

WHICH LINER?

Liquid liner: Requires practice, but lasts longest.

Pencil: Easiest to control and can be blended into a very natural look.

• Roll the point of your pencil between your fingers and let your body heat soften the pigment so that the pencil will not drag the eye.

• You only have ten to fifteen seconds after applying pencil to "smudge" for a soft effect. That's how long it takes for the liner to set.

• To get a very precise line, chill the pencil for an hour before use.

• Pencils containing silicone have the longest wearability.

HINT: If you're nervous about using eyeliner for fear of looking overdone, dampen the tip of an eyeliner wand and dip it into a deep eyeshadow. Rim the eyes for a soft look.

THE PERFECT LASH

The final touch to your eye makeup is the lash. Try to always use an eyelash curler. It will make your eyes look wider, more alert, and more youthful. It's like an instant eye lift. Always curl lashes before applying mascara.

• Lightly powder lashes to give mascara a coat to cling to.

• Heat eyelash curler with hair dryer for a few seconds. It will act like a curling iron for the eyes.

HINT: Curl twice for a rounded curl. Place the open curler near the lash roots and arrange your lashes between the two rims. Squeeze gently for thirty seconds. Squeeze again at mid-lash for another thirty seconds. It looks very natural.

• Give upper lashes a second coat of mascara, concentrating on the tips by stroking the brush horizontally across the lash. Never wait when applying second coat of mascara to lashes.

Mascara, especially waterproof mascara, dries quickly and can clump.

• Lightly coat lower lashes.

WAKEN SLEEPY EYES

Apply navy mascara over your regular mascara, concentrating on the tips and outer corners. If you don't have navy mascara, simply dip your regular mascara into blue eye shadow and coat.

HINT: Mascara now offers so much more than just color. Look for these features when choosing a mascara.

Curling Mascaras: These mascaras have an elastic quality. As the lashes dry, they shrink slightly, and flip up.

Combing Mascaras: Lash combs help with clumps. Use the comb immediately following each coat.

BLUSH

I've seen women looking absolutely glowing by using blush, while others look like they're hoping to get jobs as circus clowns. Blush can be your best beauty tool or your worst enemy. It all comes down to application. If you see lines or streaks of color on your face, you've got too much on or you haven't blended.

• Smile, and then apply blush to the apples of the cheeks. This looks more natural than running a big stripe up the side of the face. Blush is not intended to be used as a contour.

HINT: Another way to find exactly where to place blush is to turn your head upside down for a few seconds. When your head comes up, you'll see exactly where your blush should go.

HINT: To create the illusion of higher cheekbones, use a facial powder four shades darker than your natural skin tone. Apply it under the bone.

• Cream blush should be applied before powder.

HINT: Using bronzing powder as a blush will create a natural, healthy look.

• Coordinate cheek color with your lipstick, but don't go too far from the natural flush of your skin color.

• Never apply powder blush to a freshly washed face. It will look blotchy.

• Blush should never extend farther than the pupil or lower than the tip of the nose. Sweeping blush all over can appear fake and aging.

HINT: For an all-over, natural-looking glow, dip a powder brush in blush, then in face powder. Brush over entire face, concentrating on forehead, cheeks, nose, and chin.

HINT: **Blush can give your eyes a lovely glow. You can use any color except the brightest pink. Use a small brush all over the eyelid.**

Touching Up

When touching up blush during the day, apply sparingly. Your skin will have accumulated oil since you first applied your makeup, and extra blush will deepen it. If re-applying a dark blush, mix with powder.

LIP TIPS

To keep lips going all day, first pencil all over lips with a soft lip pencil. Apply lipstick over and blot.

To make lips look fuller, line lips with a pencil and then blend the edges with a sponge applicator. Cover with gloss or petroleum jelly.

To keep lipstick off teeth, pucker lips into an extreme "O". Cover your finger with a tissue, and poke it into your mouth. Slowly twist it out of your mouth, eliminating any excess color.

To achieve a pouty, sexy mouth, emphasize your top lip by dabbing just a touch of gloss in the center.

Highlight your lips with a very light eye shadow color that coordinates with your lip color tones. Place it right in the center of your upper and lower lips.

To balance unevenly shaped lips, use a lighter-colored lipstick on the smaller-sized lip.

To keep lipstick in place while dining, keep lips off utensils. Use your lower teeth and tongue to do the work.

Gently rub a washcloth over lips before applying lipstick to smooth out lips.

Apply foundation around lips to give a precise look without lip liner.

Full Lips

Lucky you if you've been blessed with those large lips women everywhere are trying to replicate with collagen. But large lips can take over your face if you're not careful.

• You really don't need lip liner, but if you like the look, soften the edge with your finger or a Q-tip.

• Don't wear any lip color that is too glossy or shiny.

Thin Lips

• Draw slightly beyond the lip with a neutral-colored lip pencil. Then apply your lipstick. Your lipstick will "catch" onto the liner.

• Apply white shadow on center of lips over lipstick and spread slightly.

• Don't wear a very dark shade of lipstick. It makes lips look smaller.

Expert Tricks

Mix petroleum jelly and blush together to create a long-lasting lip stain.

Create your own lips colors with a lip brush, a small pot, and two or three colors.

If your lips tend to bleed, use a neutral lip pencil around lips before filling in with lipstick.

To soften lip color, apply petroleum jelly over lipstick.

Blend lip liner and lipstick together on the back of the hand for a long-lasting look.

Some lipsticks can be used on the eyelids as a sheer shadow.

What's in My Lipstick?

Lipsticks have three basic components.

Pigment: Determines color.

Emollients: Carry pigment to the lips.

Waxes: Give lipstick its shape.

Lipstick Variations

Matte: This is the most lasting formula, yielding a flat coverage. Choose one that is not too drying.

Creamy: Looks best when first applied. Gives the most even coverage. Widest variety of colors.

Frosted: Shimmery coloring, containing mica.

Gloss/Stains: Generally contain moisturizers. Gives only a hint of color. Wears off most naturally and discreetly. Most likely to have added sunscreen.

Transfer-Resistant: The longest lasting lipstick available today, lasting up to eight hours.

Follow the Dots

Apply lip pencil in dots around the lip, then play "connect the dots" following the natural lip line.

LIP BLUNDER

The biggest mistake women make is wearing a lip liner that is too dark. This creates an obvious line around the mouth when lipstick wears down. Use a neutral lip liner or match your lipstick exactly!

Use Your Lipstick to Whiten Your Teeth

Change your shade of lipstick and brighten your smile. If you have a gray tinge to your teeth, wear warm shades like bronze and copper. To whiten yellow teeth, choose blue-based shades of red, raspberry, and wine.

Layer Your Lips

Keep your lipstick on all day through layering.

1. Apply lip balm.

2. Line your lips with pencil.

3. Apply lip color.

4. Blot with tissue.

5. Hold a one ply tissue over the lips and brush loose powder over lip area.

6. Press lips together to absorb powder.

Create a Frosted Look

Using your finger, smooth an iridescent eye shadow over your matte lipstick.

Lip Colors

Brown: Look for lighter formulas now available so most every woman can wear brown. Browns look best on medium to dark skin.

Pink: Gone are the bubble gum pinks. Rose pinks give a delightful glow to the face.

CORRECTIVE MAKEUP
Wide/Uneven Nose

1. Using a foundation that's one shade lighter than your natural skin tone, draw a line down the center of your nose with a sponge or your finger.

2. Shade in the side of the nose with a foundation one shade darker than your regular shade.

Scar Cover-Up

1. Dip a small brush into a cream concealer and fill in the scar.

2. Use a damp sponge to apply foundation over, blending well.

OVERPLUCKED BROWS

1. Starting with a brow pencil slightly lighter than your natural shade, draw over existing brow line, using short upward strokes.

2. Dip a stiff brush into an eye shadow that closely matches brow.

3. Press over penciled area, dabbing the color between brow hairs.

4. Lightly brush brows up with a clean mascara wand sprayed with gel to set.

MAKING UP WITH GLASSES

How you wear your makeup depends on what kind of optical prescription you have.

Nearsighted

Glasses to correct nearsightedness make eyes look smaller. Shiny eye shadow combined with liquid or cake eyeliner with at least two coats of mascara will bring eyes to the focus. Don't forget to curl lashes for that wide-eyed look.

Farsighted

The lense in this type of prescription actually magnifies the eye and makes it look disproportionately larger. Less eye makeup is called for. Use a matte eye shadow and a soft pencil in a neutral color. Go easy on the mascara. One coat is plenty.

PUTTING ON MAKEUP IN THE WRONG LIGHT IS LIKE GETTING DRESSED IN THE DARK.

1. Install 25-watt incandescent bulbs around your bathroom mirror.

2. Place a lamp on either side of your makeup mirror to eliminate shadows.

3. Apply makeup on a light-colored surface to reflect light.

4. Hold a mirror by a bright window before heading out.

HINT: To get an even application of eye makeup, don't look straight into the mirror. Position your mirror at a 45-degree angle to your chin. It will be just below chin-level. When you look down into it, you'll be able to see more of the eye to get better coverage.

QUICK MAKEUP

The Three-Minute Face

1. Apply foundation as a concealer on shadows and imperfections.

2. Coat eyelid with one neutral-colored shadow.

3. Apply liner/shadow over and under lids.

4. Use a coordinating lipstick on lips and cheeks.

5. Curl and mascara eyelashes.

6. Powder.

The One-Minute Face

1. Apply tinted moisturizer all over face.

2. Coat eyelashes with a curling mascara.

3. Apply bronzing gel on eyes, lips, and cheeks.

30-Second Makeup

Apply lip tint on eyelids, cheeks, and lips.

BRONZERS

The most versatile cosmetic you can own is a bronzer. It gives a healthy glow to the face. Many of you tell me that you stay away from bronzers because you don't like the "fake" look. Bronzers used to come in just one shade, a phony looking tan. Fortunately, there are a great variety of bronzers sold today. So how do you choose? Don't go any further than one shade darker than your regular blush. If you're prone to dry skin, pick a liquid bronzer. If you have oily skin, choose a bronzing powder. Use bronzer on the apples of your cheeks, nose, and chin. Use a big brush and apply bronzer all over the face, neck, and shoulders for a dramatic effect.

NATURAL COSMETICS

Just because a product says "natural" on the packaging is no guarantee that it doesn't contain synthetic irritants. Even those products made only from plant extracts can still cause skin reactions. Always test a cosmetic on the inner forearm.

CREATING A SULTRY FACE

Got a hot date? Have you secretly always wanted to be that Cosmo girl? Here's how to create the look.

1. Mix iridescent powder into bronzing gel and apply all over face.

2. Line upper and lower lash lines with a dark brown kohl pencil, drawing all the way into the corners of the eyes. Go over the pencil with a dark brown shadow. Continue the shadow into the crease of the eye.

3. Curl your lashes, then glue a lash strip into the outer edges of the eye.

4. Apply a cream or gel blush to the apples of the cheek for a dewy look.

5. Create sexy lips by first lining the lips with a nude pencil, then going over the lip with a sheer gloss. The look is naturally pouty.

COSMETIC SOLUTIONS

PROBLEM

Unsightly zit

SOLUTION

Turn it into a beauty mark with a brown eyeliner pencil.

PROBLEM

Blotchy foundation

SOLUTION

Avoid using a sponge to put it on. Use your fingers. Sponges remove makeup as it is applied.

PROBLEM

Smudged mascara

SOLUTION

Soak a Q-tip in makeup remover and dot on the area.

Prevent future smudges by holding a tissue under the lower lash when using mascara, and powdering under eye area.

PROBLEM

Loose powder makes a mess

SOLUTION

Spray a little hairspray on powder puff before using.

PROBLEM

Crow's feet

SOLUTION

Apply eye gel to area and set for five minutes. Make wrinkles less noticeable with a light-reflecting cream-to-powder foundation.

 HINT: Never use powder around wrinkles. It only accentuates them.

MAKEUP QUESTIONS

How can I use pastel shadows during the day?

You can wear blue, pink, and even yellow shades of eye shadow at the most conservative office if you first coat the entire eye with the pastel shade, and follow up by applying a neutral taupe or gray in the crease of your eyelid. In this way, the pastel shade will light up your eye while still looking sophisticated.

Is there any way to create cheekbones?

There are two easy ways to give the illusion of cheekbones if you can't see yours.

1. Use cream blush. It is virtually fool-proof. Lightly dot it on the apples of your cheeks and bring it up toward the hairline.

2. With a small blush brush, dust some white shadow on the cheekbone. Follow up with a light brown blusher or bronzing powder directly under it. Blend lightly together.

I like the look of liner, but it makes my eyes look smaller. What am I doing wrong?

You're most likely using a liner that's too dark. If you're using black, switch to a medium or taupe brown. You also may be drawing a line that's too thick. Practice drawing a thinner line, and don't draw the line across the entire eye. Try using the liner at the outer edges only.

How do I coordinate colors on my face?

The most modern look is the same color tones on the face. Blue eye shadow, pink cheeks, and brown lipstick looks like a beauty disaster. If you can't decide what color scheme to use, first apply lipstick. It will make the decision easy.

Is there an easy way to pluck curly eyebrows?

The problem with plucking curly brows is yanking too many hairs at one time or pulling the wrong ones. Try dabbing on some styling gel first to straighten them and make them easier to grab.

Is there any cosmetic that merits its price?

If you have a difficult time getting foundation to match your skin, then you may need to spend the money to get your color custom blended at the cosmetic counter.

How can I shorten the appearance of my nose?

To give the illusion of a shorter nose, apply foundation in a shade slightly darker than your skin tone just under the tip of the nose. Follow up with your regular shade of foundation on the rest of your face.

What can I do to take the emphasis away from my drooping eyelids?

Use a cream shadow in a neutral shade over the entire lid. Draw a sideways "V" with a dark shadow on the outer half of the eye. Blend color inward along the crease. Line eye extending up slightly at the corner.

How do I choose an eye shadow?

Don't try to match your eye color. That concept upstages your eyes. Consider your skin tone and hair color. The lighter your skin, the more understated and neutral your eye shadow.

When I line my eyebrows, I end up looking like Joan Crawford. How can I achieve a more natural look?

You should discontinue using any eyebrow liner, and just accentuate your brows with an eye shadow that is close to your brow's color.

Is there any way I can curl my lashes without a curler? I keep taking out too many eyelashes no matter what type I use.

There are a couple things to try. Run a metal spoon under warm water and press it to your lashes for at least thirty seconds. You also might try some of the curling mascaras that have become popular.

What can I do about my puffy eyes?

Try to prevent the puffiness by sleeping with two pillows to keep your head elevated. Keep baby teething rings in the freezer and apply to eyes for ten minutes. Apply hemorrhoid cream to area, tapping it in gently (as if you were playing a piano). Trace indentation just below bags with a light concealer to draw attention away from bags.

My lips droop down. Is there any way to camouflage this?

Besides cheating "up" by drawing your pencil line inside the droop, try dotting foundation on the area of the lip that drops down. Blend with a sponge, and finish off by applying lipstick inside the line you've created.

Is there anything I can do to disguise red marks on my face?

Take a yellow eye shadow and mix it with your foundation, moisturizer, or concealer. Pat or brush it into the area. The more yellow you use, the more effective the coverage. Then, gently pat powder over it to set.

Chapter 8

HAPPY HAIR

THE MANE EVENT

It's called your crowning glory for a good reason. Unless your hair is looking good, it doesn't matter how expensive your outfit, or how elaborate your makeup. Your look is not going to come together. Hard to handle hair is your No. 1 beauty complaint. It's too curly, too frizzy, too dry, too oily, etc. The point is, although everyone's hair is unique, there is a universality to hair problems and solutions.

FINDING A STYLIST

Locating a great hairstylist is like finding that pot of gold. But how do you know where to go, who to trust?

• Ask a friend or even someone you pass on the street whose hair looks great.

• Book with a nationally known salon, but ask for an appointment with their "master stylist." It will cost you a bit more, but will ensure that you get a stylist with extra training and experience.

• If you're finished in less than thirty minutes, move on. That's a rush job.

• Take a picture with you. Your stylist is not a mind reader. Don't go in and start talking about wanting Heather Locklear's hair color or Jennifer Aniston's style. That's too vague.

SHAMPOO SAVVY

The type of shampoo you use can greatly affect the condition of your hair. You can use your daily shampoo to treat your hair so that it will have more volume, shine, and manageability. You can create great shampoos at home, or with the addition of just one or two ingredients, turn the most inexpensive shampoos into multi-task miracle workers.

To Thicken

Add a packet of gelatin to ¼ cup shampoo.

Mix ½ cup white vinegar with ½ cup lemon juice. Leave on fifteen minutes, wrapping hair in a hot towel. Use ½ bottle of flat beer to rinse out. Shampoo and condition.

To Shine

Add ¼ cup of vodka to ¼ cup shampoo.

Add ¼ cup lemon juice to ½ cup water for light hair and add ¼ cup vinegar to ½ cup water for dark hair. Use both as a final rinse after using regular conditioner.

To Strengthen

Mix an egg into your regular shampoo. Leave on for five to ten minutes. Rinse.

HINT: Rinse in lukewarm water. Hot water could scramble the egg right in your hair.

Alternate Shampoos

Every two or three weeks, you should change your shampoo. Your hair will let you know when it's time.

• It will feel weighed down after shampooing.

• You hair will be difficult to style.

• Your hair is dull.

HINT: Avoid alcohol in hair products. It can dry out hair, and is no longer necessary as a stabilizing component.

HINT: To get hair squeaky clean, mix 1 tablespoon baking soda with two teaspoons shampoo.

PROPER SHAMPOOING

• Use your fingertips, not your nails, to wash your hair.

• Use lukewarm, not hot, water to wash and rinse.

• Massage your scalp to encourage hair growth. It will also rid the scalp of residue product, which inhibits growth.

HAIR MYTH

Daily shampooing will make hair fall out.

REALITY

Although aggressive shampooing can cause breakage, a clean scalp can actually encourage hair growth by keeping buildup from occurring.

THE SCALP
is the only area of the body that doesn't have muscle directly beneath it. Consequently, this area has less blood circulation.

TREATMENT

FRIZZY HAIR

Mash an avocado with an egg yolk. Work into hair and leave in for at least fifteen minutes. Rinse out and shampoo and condition as usual.

DRY HAIR

Add two tablespoons mayonnaise to ½ teaspoon honey. Massage into hair and leave on ten to fifteen minutes. Sit in the sun or under the hair dryer to intensify the treatment. Rinse with seltzer water. Shampoo and condition.

Apply ½ cup whipped cream to hair. Leave on thirty minutes. Rinse and shampoo.

DANDRUFF AND DRY SCALP
Do You Have Dandruff or a Dry Scalp?

Dandruff is bacteria on the scalp. It starts at the hairline, and it is usually extremely itchy. Dry scalp is just that, and can sometimes be caused by hair products.

Dandruff Treatment

Dip a cotton ball in castor oil. Rub it in the scalp and hairline areas to dissolve flakes. Leave on for ten minutes before washing out.

Mix ¼ cup witch hazel with ¼ cup mouthwash. Spritz onto just-washed hair. Mouthwash is an antiseptic that kills germs. Witch hazel is a natural astringent that controls oil.

Massage scalp with sea salt. It acts as a natural exfoliant.

Dissolve five aspirin in ⅓ cup shampoo.

Add one teaspoon rosemary to two tablespoons olive oil. Leave on ten minutes.

Vitamin E capsules as well as vitamin E oil, rubbed into the scalp will eliminate flakes.

Aloe vera gel, applied with a cotton ball into the scalp, acts immediately. Let it set for about five minutes, shampoo, and rinse.

Dry Scalp Remedy

Mix two drops of vanilla extract with two tablespoons whole mayonnaise. Massage into scalp, and wrap entire head in aluminum foil. Leave on for fifteen minutes. Wash out completely.

THE ULTIMATE STYLER

Flat beer is the hair styling secret from behind the runways and top pageants. It's kept a secret, because not many would admit to pouring unglamorous flat beer all over their heads. But it's been used for years because it works. It styles without sticking, and nothing gives better bounce.

Pour about a ½ cup flat beer in a mister (available at drugstores and beauty supply stores). Spray on freshly washed hair before setting or styling. Don't worry about the odor, it evaporates.

Beer also gives life to a tired perm or naturally curly hair that tends to droop. Spritz the beer on dry hair, and scrunch the style into shape.

ENVIRONMENTALLY SAFE HAIRSPRAY

Dissolve a tablespoon of sugar into a glass of hot water. Allow it to cool, and use it in a spray bottle.

A MODEL'S SECRET

Ever wonder what makes those models' hair extensions look so real? Hairstylists rub their hair with big balloons to create static electricity, letting the hair settle naturally.

HAIR PROBLEMS AND SOLUTIONS

DAMAGED HAIR

Mash a ripe banana, blending in a few drops of almond oil. Massage over entire head and leave on for fifteen minutes. Rinse with seltzer water. Shampoo and condition.

Distribute two teaspoons sesame oil and ½ cup yogurt evenly over hair and scalp. Wrap in foil to contain heat. Leave on thirty minutes. Wash thoroughly and apply a leave-in conditioner.

FINE, LIMP HAIR

To create extra body, use a volumizing spray at the roots before blow-drying. Use a large round brush at least two inches in diameter. Keep brush at roots, rather than the ends when blow-drying. Finish by setting the crown in velcro rollers.

HINT: Don't use too much product if your hair is fine. It only weighs it down.

Get the Look of Fullness

Have your stylist create a few lowlights to create the illusion of volume.

Volumizing Pear Hair Pack

Run a Bosc pear under warm water to soften. (You can also use canned pears, and there will be no need to soften.) Peel and remove seeds. Place pear in a bowl and mash with a fork. Mix in one teaspoon plain gelatin. Apply mixture to just-washed hair, massaging into scalp and working throughout hair. Leave on for fifteen minutes. Shampoo thoroughly. Pears contain tannins, which give hair astounding texture and volume.

SLEEP IN VOLUME

Sweep your hair into a high ponytail. Sleep with it in, and in the morning your hair will have lots of volume.

HAIR KINKS

When wavy hair develops kinks, run a coat of silicone-based anti-frizz serum all over the hair. Use a large round brush and blow dry. Be sure to hold hair taut.

DARK ROOTS

If you find yourself with unsightly roots, and there's no time to re-color, there are techniques that will camouflage the problem.

Commercially Made Crayon Sticks and Sprays

These are sold in most beauty supply stores and some drugstores.

Eye Shadow

Powdered eye shadows come in so many colors, it's easy to get an exact match to most hair shades. Use makeup remover or cold cream and wipe off before shampooing out.

Rollers

Put a few rollers around the roots and crown to add height. This will lift hair from the scalp and hide roots.

Criss-Cross Part

Make an uneven, zig-zag line around part line.

GREASY HAIR

Rub a piece of tissue paper on your scalp. If you can see oil on the tissue, treat accordingly.

Check your shampoo. It could be creating residue on your hair. Once a week, pour ½ cup of an astringent like Sea Breeze on your head. Massage it in, and leave it on for ten minutes. Rinse thoroughly.

Oily Hair Tonic

1 egg

½ cup milk

2 tablespoons lemon juice

Combine and massage into scalp. Wrap head in aluminum foil for thirty minutes. Rinse in apple cider vinegar.

Apple Polish

The pectin in apple juice absorbs excess oil, leaving hair squeaky clean. In a bowl, combine ⅓ cup apple juice with ½ teaspoon white vinegar. Pour over freshly washed hair. Leave on for fifteen minutes. Rinse out with seltzer water. The vinegar intensifies the apple juice's oil-absorbing power.

NO TIME TO SHAMPOO

You can quickly absorb grease by sprinkling baby powder at your roots, then combing through. Be careful not to use too much powder, or you'll look like you have gray hair.

Dab facial toner over scalp with a cotton ball. Blow dry.

FADING HAIR COLOR

Be careful about the hair color you're using.

Dandruff shampoos are so notorious for stripping hair color they're often recommended for removing excess color to over-processed hair. Choose a gentle non-alkaline shampoo. (Baby shampoo is a good choice.) If you have dandruff, make up your own dandruff treatment.

Dissolve thirty aspirin in a full-sized bottle of inexpensive shampoo. This treatment does not require refrigeration, and will not strip hair color. It's used on several television series where actors must keep their hair color intact, and was given to me by one of Hollywood's top hairstylists to the stars, Dusty Fleming.

• Don't wash hair for at least two days after coloring so that it will lock in.

• Always rinse in tepid water. Hot water speeds color fading by opening hair cuticles.

SPLIT ENDS

Separate a two-inch section of dry hair and twist the strand from scalp to end. If you can see pieces sticking out, then you have split ends.

Hair breakage is most often caused by aggressively brushing wet hair.

• Use a wide-tooth comb and gently comb through the ends before combing entire head.

• Don't hold your blow-dryer too close to your hair, and keep it moving.

GROWING OUT A STYLE

It's frustrating when hair gets to that in-between stage. Whether you're growing out bangs or an entire hairstyle, those pesky pieces seem to have a mind of their own.

• Use barrettes and hair accessories.

• Knots and braids can provide a fun look if you can carry it off.

• Strong gel will disguise strands and give them a "piecey" look.

HINT: Use nettle tea to promote hair growth. Brew up a strong tea and pour over clean, wet hair. Leave on ten minutes. Rinse out.

BRASSY HAIR COLOR

Mix a bottle of hair toner with 1½ ounces water, and ½ ounce 20-volume peroxide. Pour over hair, covering entire head. Leave on ten minutes, and then shampoo out.

HAT HAIR

Turn your head upside down and rub roots vigorously, running fingers throughout hair. Mist with hairspray while head is upside down.

TIGHT HAIR

Go over hair gently with a dryer. The heat will loosen the curl.

BIG HAIR

When it's very humid outside, hair that's curly or wavy can go all over the place and create too much volume. Apply a leave-in conditioner which will weigh down the hair just enough.

MAKE THE MOST OF YOUR HAIR PRODUCTS

USE LESS

Start with just a fingertip, and always rub product in the palms of your hands before massaging it into your hair. So many women pour their shampoos directly from the bottle into their hair. It not only is a terrible waste of money and product, but you're more apt to get an uneven application.

READ LABELS AND FOLLOW INSTRUCTIONS

Some products are meant to work while hair is damp, while others work best on dry hair.

HINT: Check ingredients to choose the right product for your hair type.

HAIR TYPES
Fine Hair

Ingredients to look for: wheat proteins and polymers. They coat the hair shaft, making it appear thicker.

Dry Hair

Ingredients to look for: silk amino acids adds softness and repairs hair structure. Lecithin restores hair texture.

CLEAN YOUR HAIR DRYER

Use an old toothbrush to clean your hair dryer's filter. You'll find that your hair dryer will perform more efficiently.

ADDING SHINE

Fine Hair

Learn to use spray volumizers. They are light enough to deposit a light mist of shine droplets on the hair without wilting it.

Normal Hair

Gels and creams will add shine without weight. First, it's necessary to pour the product in your palm. Rub your hands together, and then lightly pat over head.

Thick, Coarse Hair

The best shine enhancers for this type of hair are old-fashioned pomades. They work not only to deliver shine, but to moisturize this type of hair.

Strawberry Hair Mask

Mash eight strawberries with one tablespoon mayonnaise. Massage into washed, damp hair. Cover with a shower cap, then a warm towel. Wash out with a shampoo/conditioner combination. This luscious mix of rich acidic berries will leave your hair both conditioned and with rich gloss.

Tips for More Shine

• Use heat-activated shampoo.

• Deep condition at least weekly.

• Don't use too many styling products that can dull the hair by coating it.

CHECK YOUR WATER

If your hair has continued to look dull and life-less no matter what products you've tried, the culprit could be your water. Hard water contains minerals, which build up on hair.

Test

Fill two glasses, one with bottled water and one from your tap. Add one tablespoon dishwashing detergent to both. Stir until suds form. If less suds form in tap water, then it is hard. Try using bottled water as a final rinse when you shampoo.

HAIR AS CAMOUFLAGE

You can use your hairstyle to help you solve some of your beauty dilemmas.

CROW'S FEET AND FOREHEAD WRINKLES

Long, piecey bangs will soften lines around the eyes while covering wrinkles.

CREPEY NECK

Ask your stylist to layer around your face, angling at and below the chin.

WEAR BANGS, BUT KEEP THEM LIGHT

Your stylist should be able to cut into your bangs to keep them light and wispy. Heavy bangs bring unneeded attention to wrinkles and crow's feet.

FULL FACE

A good stylist can take pounds off your face with the right haircut.

Layers are the most important tool a stylist can use in slenderizing the face. Full cheeks become sculpted by creating angles starting at the temple and ending just below the cheekbones.

A **round face** can be lengthened by creating wispy bangs cut in an upside down "v" pattern. The shortest section of the bang will be at the center of the forehead.

Double chins can be easily camouflaged by beginning layering at the jawbone just below the ear lobe. Finish layering just below the chin.

Blow-drying hair on a large round brush directly

onto the face reduces width, frames your best features, and is extremely sexy.

An elegantly **upswept hairdo** with loosely gathered tendrils around the face brings attention away from the body.

Highlights create long vertical lines, and the illusion of slimness.

Height in the crown of the head will instantly lengthen the face.

Consider **lightening** your hair by a shade or two. It will open up the face, and instantly slim down cheekbones.

DON'T LET YOUR HAIR AGE YOU

WATCH YOUR COLOR

The rules to coloring your hair is not to go too light or too dark. Too dark is too severe for the aging face. When the face ages, it loses pigment. Women who lighten their hair too much will end up using a lot of color in their face to make up for the loss of color. Bright, vibrant shades are more flattering to the face.

GET THE RIGHT CUT

I've seen women who add years when they don't have to by wearing stiff, overdone hairdos. Loosening up with a soft, modern cut can chop the years off.

TIME SAVERS

PRODUCTS

Shampoos with conditioners provide one-step cleaning.

Hair fresheners get rid of odor when there's no time to shampoo.

Quick dry shampoos that contain proteins and acids minimize water absorption.

◀▶ **HINT: Although it saves time on a rinse, don't use leave-in conditioner unless you have extremely dry or damaged hair. Leave-in conditioners tend to make the hair lose body.**

QUICK LOOKS

Even if there's no time to shampoo, you can create a new look at every hair length.

• If you have short hair, use your hands to style and shape.

• Medium length hair will take on a a highly sophisticated appearance when slicked back.

• There are some exciting new accessories that allow long-haired beauties options beyond just pulling it back. Barrettes, headbands, and clips are now widely available.

SALON TIPPING ETIQUETTE

STYLIST: If you love the results: 20 to 25 percent. Passable, but not great: 15 percent

SALON OWNER: Not necessary to tip. Clients might bring in bagels or muffins.

SHAMPOO PERSON: $2.00 to $5.00. The more the shampoo person helps with treatments and blow-drying, the higher the tip.

WHAT DOES THAT PRODUCT DO?

STATIC SOLUTIONS

• Run a fabric softener sheet over your hair, or enmesh it in your brush.

• Spray Static Guard directly on your brush.

• Run hand lotion over hair.

• Spray leave-in conditioner on dry hair.

• Combine ¼ cup liquid fabric softener with ¼ cup water. Spritz on hair.

CURL AND WAVE REVIVER

Mix equal amounts of water and conditioner into a spritzer bottle. Spray into hair and shake head. Let air dry.

CURL DIFFUSER

Direct air flattens curl, so if your dryer did not come with a diffuser, make your own by securing the top part of panty hose with an elastic band on the end of your blow-dryer.

FRIED HAIR

Rub almond oil over dry hair to add shine without build up.

CURLS

GET SPIRAL CURLS WITHOUT A PERM

The first time I saw a hairstylist coming at me with a kitchen fork, I didn't know what to think. However, I have been in this business long enough to not judge until I've seen the results. This is one even I didn't believe, but the curl holds, even in the straightest hair. Try it yourself.

Take a fork, and pick up about an inch of hair. Wrap it around the fork (just like you would spaghetti). Spray it with hairspray and blow it dry. The heat from the metal in the fork creates a long-lasting spiral curl. Use it for a few curls for effect, or over entire head.

HINT: If you have longed for curls, but were born stiff-straight, ask your stylist about Helix shears. With these special scissors, your stylist can give your hair curl and volume without any chemicals.

CURL MAINTENANCE

Whether curly hair is permed or natural, it needs protection against the elements.

1. Rely on leave-in conditioner to make it less prone to frizz and easier to manage. Curly hair frizzes easily because of its coarse texture.

2. For best results, curly hair should be combed, not brushed. When possible, hair should be dried naturally.

STYLING SECRETS

SHORT HAIR TIP

Use a toothbrush to tease short strands. The tiny bristles will give you more control, and give hair more lift.

BLOW-DRYING

1. Blow-dry bangs first, since they are first to dry. Use a round brush.

2. Use fingers to separate hair until almost dry.

3. Divide hair into sections, and dry bottom sections first.

HINT: Always brush and blow-dry in the same direction.

TRIM YOUR OWN BANGS

1. Comb bangs straight down across your forehead.

2. Separate into three sections.

3. Clip back the two side sections.

4. Grasp the middle section between fingers, and looking straight ahead cut off about ¼ inch.

5. Unclip side sections and repeat.

SLEEP ON SATIN

Keep your hair from losing its style overnight by always sleeping on a satin pillow. Carry one with you when you travel.

PROTECTING YOUR HAIR

POOL PROTECTION

Swimming pools can ruin hair. The chlorine in a pool is a strong bleach. It will discolor hair and leave it with an unattractive green tinge. Protect your hair before going in by applying a deep conditioner. Immediately after, rinse your hair in apple cider vinegar, then with club soda. The carbonation will lift excess salt and chlorine out.

SUN PROTECTION

It's impossible and impractical to wear head protection in the sun. Protect your hair by mixing ½ cup water with ½ teaspoon 25 SPF sunscreen. Spritz on damp hair before styling.

Apply sunscreen to the part in your hair. If you find it too messy, then use a lip balm which has a high SPF factor.

SUN-PROOFING COLOR

If you're blonde or brunette, go half a shade darker, knowing that the color will fade. If you're a redhead, use a color-locking gloss treatment.

IS YOUR HAIR DRYER DRYING OR FRYING?

Set your dryer on high and direct it about three inches from your hand. If it starts to become too uncomfortable to remain in that position before you count to five, the setting is too hot for your hair.

Set dryer on high and direct it about four inches from a mirror. If you can see a red reflection in the mirror, then it's too hot.

HAIRSTYLIST SPEAK

Do you know what you're going to get when you visit a hair salon. The next time a stylist throws a term at you, you'll know exactly what to expect.

LOWLIGHTS

Darkens sections of the hair.

TAPERED

Gradually slants hair from short to long.

LAYERING

Cutting hair in different lengths. It's done to create movement and volume.

HAIR TRENDS

THE WET LOOK

I love this trend. It makes hair glisten! To get it, mash together ¼ cup olive oil and one-half very ripe avocado and apply to hair. Wrap your head in aluminum foil and then let it sit for thirty minutes. Shampoo out.

HINT: Mix gel and conditioner together for a less stiff, more moisturized look.

CRUNCHY HAIR

To get that piecey look of hard, separated hair seen on the runways, you need to run for your salt shaker. Add two teaspoons of salt to ¼ cup almond oil. Spritz on hair and let dry.

COLOR GALORE

AT-HOME COLORING TIPS

You can get really great results with the new home-coloring products. They have become so easy to use that they're practically foolproof, and ever so natural-looking.

• Deep condition before you color.

• Wait two days after shampooing before coloring. The color will adhere better, and since your scalp is more sensitive after shampooing, it will make the process more comfortable. Plus the natural oils in your hair will protect it.

HINT: Here's a bizarre secret to getting hair color off your hands and around the hairline. Rub the stains with wet cigarette ashes.

NATURAL HAIR COLORING
Dark Hair

Dark-haired beauties can create a temporary color with tea, walnuts, and coffee.

• Brew a strong tea and use as a final rinse. Boil one cup of chopped walnuts with one cup water. Strain the liquid and pour over head. Leave on thirty minutes before shampooing. Brew an espresso or other strong coffee. Add to dry hair. Leave on thirty minutes before shampooing out. This will add sparkling highlights to black or dark brown hair.

• Combine ½ cup vinegar with ¼ cup soy sauce to give highlights and subtle coloring to dark hair. The soy sauce not only has protein for strength, but also brown pigment. Leave on fifteen to twenty minutes. Wash out thoroughly.

• Use ½ cup cranberry juice as final rinse to enhance red hair or create subtle red highlights to dark hair.

Light Hair

Brew a cup of very strong chamomile tea. Let it cool to lukewarm. Spray or comb into dry hair. Leave on twenty minutes (if possible sit in the sun). Shampoo and rinse. This gives a color lift and subtle highlights to blonde and light brown hair.

HAIR MYTH

Hair color is harmful.

REALITY

There have been numerous studies done that have found no significant risk to indicate that any hair color raises cancer risks. If this issue is of particular concern, use one of the new vegetable, nontoxic colors available at most salons.

HAIR QUESTIONS

How do I keep my hair from looking like a helmet?

You're probably drying your hair with a round brush that's too small for your style. Try switching to a vent brush. You'll get the height you want without the tightness.

What is the least damaging way to straighten hair, chemical straightening or ironing?

If you've been straightening with an iron on a daily basis (many models do), getting a chemical straightening will be much less harmful than "frying" your hair daily . That said, before having your hair chemically straightened, get a good cut and deep condition it for one to two weeks.

Why can't I get the same look that my hairstylist gives my hair?

If you can't manage your hair at home, the hairstyle could be too complicated, or not suitable to your hair. Go back and have your stylist teach you how to maintain it. If that doesn't work, ask for a more simple style (less layers, etc.).

Is there any way to get excess color off my hair when I've left my dye on too long?

You should wash your hair twice with a mild dishwashing detergent. There are also products sold in beauty supply stores with names indicating their use, such as Uncolor.

Chapter 9

STYLE SENSE

SECRETS OF STYLE

Style is that elusive "something" that makes a person stand out. Don't mistake it with being "fashionable." Style has nothing to do with fashion, and fashion cannot give you style. You can run out and copy every new trend that's out there, and look worse than if you ignored it all. If you take fashion too seriously, you've become a fashion victim.

KEEP YOUR WARDROBE LEAN AND MEAN

We wear 20 percent of our wardrobe 80 percent of the time.

The other 80 percent is a melange of special-occasion wear, sales too good to pass up, trends gone past, wrong size, and sentimental attachments.

Throw it out if you haven't worn it in over a year.

BUILDING A WARDROBE

Stay Classic

Trends may come and go, but you'll never be out of style if you base your wardrobe on the styles that have been around forever.

Purchase quality items and they'll be the mainstay of your wardrobe for several years.

Stay Neutral

Build your basic wardrobe in neutral shades like black, beige, navy, or brown. Don't ignore the fashion industry's "hot" colors of the season. Use them as accent pieces. If purple is "the" color, don't buy a purple coat, but do purchase a purple blouse. This is the way to be stylish without being ridiculous.

Keep It Simple

The simpler the shape, the more expensive the piece will look. Too much embellishment also gives the piece a shorter life. Add panache with accessories if your piece needs more.

Check Details

The way a garment is made should be as important to you as how it looks. Inspect everything from the way the armholes are cut to the quality of the buttons. Test the zipper to make sure it moves smoothly on the track.

Basic Black Dress

You can wear it to work with a jacket over it, and it looks professional. At night, add a little sparkling jewelry or pearls, and it's a party dress.

The White Shirt

By far, the single most timeless, seasonless must-have for your wardrobe. Look for a semi-tailored style in a medium weight. Use it under a suit during the week, and with jeans during the weekend.

The Black Skirt

It should come just at or above the knee. Dressed up with a jacket or dressed down with a tank top, it's a must-have for every wardrobe.

Basic Trouser

Choose a belted, pleated trouser to cornerstone your sportswear.

Well-Cut Jacket

Wear it with jeans or a dress. Fit and fabric are key in making your selection.

Cardigan Sweater

Select a sweater that is not too loose in size or in its stitching. Coordinate it with the basic trouser and skirt. It can substitute as a jacket.

Jeans

They're classic, classy, and flattering.

Classic Raincoat

Get one that will double as an evening coat. An oversized mid-calf version will look great over a suit, dress, or jeans.

YOU CAN AFFORD COUTURE

Purchase one or two couture pieces to bring elegance to your wardrobe. It will be well worth the investment.

YOUR CLOTHES ARE YOUR REFLECTION

Adapt your own style to the times. If you have never felt comfortable with very tailored styles, then stop stockpiling your closet with them.

DRESS LIKE A WOMAN

Pantsuits, menswear, and athletic wear looks absolutely terrible if overdone. To wear these looks and still look like a woman, add something feminine. It might be the slight touch of lace socks with athletic sneakers.

HAVE IT TAILORED

You may look fine in that outfit, but wouldn't you look even better if it was custom-fit to your shape? Many women are surprised to find that tailoring is not nearly as expensive as they had imagined. Plus, it can give new life to out-of-date clothing.

SHOPPING SAVVY

- Go to the stores with the largest inventory. A major department store will also have the largest markdown selection.

- Don't buy it unless you have something to wear with it.

- Make sure you can wear it all year. The seasonless fabrics are usually better quality.

- Shop by yourself. Friends are not objective, and the salesperson just wants the sale.

- Write it down. Shop with a list to avoid impulse purchases.

- Buy in quantity. If you find something that really fits and flatters, you'll never regret it. This really applies to pants, especially jeans.

- Stay away from last-minute shopping. You'll never find exactly what you want. Plus, you'll feel uncomfortable "breaking it in" at an important function.

- Shop for a designer. There are designers who dedicate themselves to a certain type of woman. It will streamline your shopping to pick two or three who suit your style.

- Buy for function as well as style.

- Choose solids over print patterns. You'll get more wearings per use.

- Calculate your cost-per-wear.

- Buy only what you love. Any seconds thoughts on an item? Then pass it by.

- Shoo away salespeople by telling them you need time to think.

- Don't set a strict budget.

- Don't shop in the same stores. Try a new mall, or stores in a new city.

FABRICS

CASHMERE

This fabric looks rich, whether paired with jeans or the most elegant skirt. The more you wash it, the softer it gets (wash in shampoo). If the price of cashmere throws you off, look for blends.

LIGHTWEIGHT WOOLS

Summer-weight wool is wearable in all but one or two months a year, giving you tremendous mileage. It drapes beautifully, and wears forever with every fabric imaginable.

LYCRA

A small percent of it can make all the difference. It will help clothing keep its shape.

LEATHER AND SUEDE

Look for soft and supple materials.

HINT: There are some very realistic faux leathers and suedes at a fraction of the price. Keep in mind that gloss cheapens the look.

ORIENTAL AND BROCADE FABRICS

These fabrics can be worn during the day with plain pieces, and go into evening with delicate fabrics and beading.

SHEER

Choose items with built-in layers and linings to look elegant and sexy, yet modest.

JERSEY

Go for heavier weight to fall elegantly. Think about going up a size to avoid cling.

DENIM

The darker the denim, the more it will work like black. Dark denim is dressier than its faded counterpart.

LINEN

Don't let the wrinkles bother you. Linen is supposed to wrinkle, and be worn wrinkled. It's part of the look and texture.

If it really bothers you, heavy starch will keep the wrinkles at bay.

WHEN AND WHERE

WHEN IN DOUBT, ADD ON

Overdressing is like an insurance card. Add a jacket to a blouse and pair of pants if you're not sure how everyone else will be dressed. It's easier to take off that jacket than to appear underdressed.

CLEAVAGE IS A DAYTIME NO

Keep those plunging necklines for after hours.

CASUAL WEAR

Also known as casual chic, it's a look that doesn't appear contrived. There's a difference between casual and sloppy. Sweatshirts belong in the gym, not the workplace.

FIT IS EVERYTHING

PANTS

For almost every woman, there is a different fit. For every pair of pants, there is a woman who can wear them. The point is, it's going to take a lot of strikes before hitting that home run. Go into those fitting rooms, and look at yourself in a three-way mirror. There are some pants that will work better than others.

• Disguise a flat rear with back pocket details.

• A protruding rear is flattered by a dropped waistline.

• Large thighs look better with pants with full-cut legs and loose waistbands.

• Large or poochy stomachs look best in pants with elastic or drawstrings.

• Women with heavy legs or who are heavy all over should look for pants in lightweight fabrics.

• Flatter thin legs with substantial fabrics and structured lining.

HINT #1: When shopping, wear the same type of shoes you'd wear with the pants you're looking for.

HINT #2: Shop on an empty stomach so your pants won't be uncomfortable while trying them on, and you'll get an accurate fit.

JACKETS

The mistake most women make is wearing a jacket that doesn't fit properly. A jacket that's too tight looks less than expensive while a jacket that's too large looks like the out-of-date "boyfriend" style of the 1980s.

• Seams should be straight and tightly sewn with no pulls or puckering.

- Go for the best fabric you can afford.

- Linings should flow with the drape of the jacket.

- Women who are top-heavy should stay away from double-breasted jackets.

- Buttons should be double enforced with extras on the inside of the jacket.

- Pocket edges should be finished with pockets that lie flat.

TOPS

Blouses, sweaters, and tunics are critical in fit because they are more visible to the eye.

- Buttons should meet button holes straight on.

- Choose armholes that no more than 1½ inches lower than the armpit. This will give a longer line.

- Consider height and proportion when choosing a tunic or sweater. A long V neck can camouflage a thick waist, elongate a short neck, and balance a short waist.

- Shoulder pads should be well-constructed and attached for cleaning.

- Natural fibers will be more comfortable, but will not keep their shape as well.

COATS

Think about a coat as a three- to four-year investment. Purchase the highest quality you can afford, in a classic style.

- You should be able to cross your arms and fit a jacket or sweater underneath comfortably.

- Look for 100 percent wool or a high wool blend. It will retain its shape, and natural fibers are better able to trap heat.

- Check the lining. The best drape will come from a fully lined coat. Sleeves also should be lined.

- Purchase a coat with buttons that can be moved easily. It's the easy way to change the fit if your weight should fluctuate.

FASHION DON'TS

Plastic Shopping Bags

Exposed Underwear

Rubber Dresses

Micro tops

Plaid pants

Mix and match patterns

Large handbags

Lace hose

Lingerie inspirations

Fashion fads the second time around

Puffed sleeves

Showing shape and skin at the same time

White hose unless you're a nurse

COLORS

Are the colors you're wearing your most flattering colors? Choose colors that harmonize with your natural coloring. They will be the colors that will enhance your appearance. If you've ever been asked if you were tired or sick when you weren't, then it's time to start experimenting.

Often, the color of the season doesn't flatter our own coloring. If you love a particular color, but it doesn't do wonderful things for your complexion, then use it as an accent piece in a handbag, shoes, or a scarf.

BODY COMFORT

Clothing should fit your body type, and you should be comfortable enough in your body where you are not relying on fashion to define your style, but to enhance it. Your personal style should be evident when you're practically wearing your birthday suit. You feel it, with and without clothing.

BODY TYPES

TRIANGLE

Lower torso is usually two to three sizes larger the than the upper half of the body.

FASHION CHOICES: Pleated pants, bright colors on top, dark pants/skirts, shoulder pads, upper body detailing.

HOURGLASS

Curvy, balanced body type with wide shoulders, defined waist, and rounded hips.

FASHION CHOICES: Average-weight hourglass bodies should accentuate this ideal body type with simple styling. Large-sized hourglass figures should avoid nipped-in waists, and choose long, free-flowing clothing.

WEDGE

This body type features broad shoulders, flat rears, straight legs, and possibly large breasts. Waists are tapered rather than defined.

FASHION CHOICES: The emphasis should be on clothing that accentuates the narrow hips of this body type. Slim skirts and long tops are good choices.

TRICKS OF THE TRADE

MIX TEXTURES

Just as we have long loved to combine high- and low-end clothing—that expensive jacket with those old jeans—mixing up textures carries that same panache.

Lacy camisole under a business suit

Leather and silk

Tee shirt and a long skirt

Sequins and cashmere

Jeans and pearls

SURPRISE MATCHING

One of the keys to the appearance of true style is to create surprise when putting together a look. Looking too matched is gone, and looking like you're trying too hard makes you look like a true victim of fashion.

RETAIL LAW

Most states protect consumers who pay full price by guaranteeing you the reduced price if the item you bought goes on sale within seven days from the time of purchase. Save your sales receipt and watch your newspapers.

SHOPPING SALES

IS IT A BARGAIN?

#1

It's something you've been looking for.

#2

It goes with at least two items in your wardrobe.

#3

It's a label you recognize.

#4

It doesn't look shop-worn.

#5

It's not orange.

WHERE TO SPEND WHERE TO SAVE

BUY IT AT FULL PRICE

Black skirt or pants

Comfortable yet stylish shoes

A great jacket

White shirt

DON'T BOTHER UNTIL IT'S ON SALE

Dress of the moment

Tee shirts

Workout wear

Dressy blouse or top

HOW TO WEAR
RUNWAY FASHION

Just because it looks great on that runway model, can you really wear it?

THE SLIP DRESS

Those sheer chiffon dresses have been seen on all the runways and celebrities. You like the look, but how can you wear it without risking arrest? Look for lined styles, or buy a slip to wear underneath. Designers are bringing slip dresses to the mainstream by giving us more opaque fabrics to choose from.

If you are not comfortable showing so much skin, consider the slip skirt. It's a feminine, sexy look with a little tank or cardigan and heels.

LACE

Choose this look in simple, sleeved shapes in cardigans, shirts, and camisoles. Layer them under fitted tops because anything bulky will ruin the look.

A floaty lace skirt with a more severe jacket is an eclectic mix that looks very modern.

RUFFLES

Too much ruffle, particularly under anything very tailored, will scream Austin Powers. A little ruffle on a skirt hem or blouse looks current.

Ruffles with jeans, capris, or slim fitting pants are a direct-from-the-runway look most women can feel comfortable in.

PRINTS

A print with a black or dark background will be most flattering and work across the seasons.

Be very careful how you wear prints. Patterns draw attention. If you have problem spots, wear them away from those areas.

QUESTIONS

Is it proper to wear leather in the summer?

Summer leathers are not only acceptable, they are the hottest thing in fashion. A white leather skirt, while looking a bit "too much" in winter, is perfect for those warmer months. Pastel leathers, as well as suedes, are just the right touch for a night on the town. Look for suede and leather halters, unlined jackets, and short-sleeved, tailored shirts to bring excitement to your summer wardrobe.

What do I wear under a backless dress?

There are backless bras that you can buy that the celebrities use when they wear those revealing, figure-hugging fashions. The bras are essentially four bras in one. They convert for halter, criss-cross, and open-style, as well as backless.

How do I know if I'm too old to wear something?

Shop by personality, body type, and the compliments you receive. The life you live and how well you've taken care of yourself influences the decision-making much more than your chronological age. I encourage women to shop stores out of their demographic. You'll get an education into what's hot, and you might just find something you'll love.

How do trends develop?

Designers show what they hope will become trends on their runways. Then it's a combination of catching department store buyers' interest with hoping a celebrity will wear their label, it will be photographed, and everyone will want it. Of course, the designers are known to try to sweeten the pot by sending the celebrity a few of their top picks when a major event comes up.

Chapter 10

WORKING STYLE

DRESSING FOR SUCCESS

The image you present at work is key to how you are perceived, the respect you get, and your chances of climbing the corporate ladder. What you wear will send an instant message that will become indelible and identify you as part of a team. Although companies have become more open, and casual Fridays have become the norm, there are still rules that may make or break your best intentions.

CLOTHES THAT WILL GET YOU HIRED

When you set out to get that job, play it safe. First impressions are most lasting. Employers have told me that once a look turned them off, it didn't matter what a candidate said.

1. You can't lose in a suit in a neutral color. Choose what you feel most comfortable in, pants or skirt. Just be sure that the skirt isn't too short, and the pants aren't too tight.

HINT: Be careful about what you wear under your suit. A low camisole is a definite no, and anything too sheer will get you nowhere. A man-tailored shirt is always appropriate if a suit is not completely closed.

2. A tailored dress is a good choice. Wear a coordinating jacket just in case. Look around you when you get to the interview. If the look is pretty casual, then take it off once you reach the interview site if that makes you more comfortable.

3. Coordinate your accessories carefully. Match your purse and shoes, and be sure to wear basic colors.

4. Keep your jewelry subtle and small. Large jewelry is not only a distraction, it makes too much noise.

5. Pay attention to details. I'm constantly reminded of the CEO who confided to me that she never hires anyone with unmanicured nails.

6. Hair should be groomed in such a way as to not be distracting. If your hair is long, pull it back or put it up. If hair is curly, tousled, or has a lot of volume, polish it down with gel or spray.

7. Check your makeup. Make sure certain colors are understated and blended. Skip the eye shadow, especially in purple.

CREATING A WORKING WARDROBE

Most new jobs call for brand-new clothes. This should call for celebration, except when there's a budget to consider. The key to an inexpensive working wardrobe is to purchase a few staples that you can mix and match to create different looks.

Basics

Pantsuit

Select a conservative suit in black, brown, or navy.

Tailored Blouses

Pick up one or two. One should be white, and then pick one in a bright color.

Skirt

Pick a dark-colored skirt to coordinate with the jacket in the pantsuit. The length should be right around the knee.

Dress Casual

Casual Fridays

Dress-down Fridays and casual attire at the office have become commonplace. But what is going too far?

Don'ts

Bare midriffs and necklines

Workout clothing

Anything too tight or too short

T-shirts with slogans

Ripped denim

Panty Hose

If you hate panty hose in the summer, rely on ankle-length skirts or pants to give you a professional look.

Shoes

A sandal that's too strappy is not appropriate in the office. Coworkers should not have to look upon each other's toes.

GROOMING ON THE JOB

Don't ever groom in public. Personal hygiene should be kept personal, and the only place to do any of it is in the rest room.

USE YOUR LUNCH HOUR TO WORK OUT

Turn your lunch hour into a better body break. You can reap big rewards with even thirty minutes of your lunch hour. You'll feel invigorated and ready to face the rest of your day.

Walk

Keep a pair of sneakers at work so you're always ready. Find a hill for extra exertion.

Join an Exercise Class

Find a fitness club near your office. Many cater to work schedules and feature lunch-time workouts.

Take Over the Conference Room

Usually left empty during the lunch hour, it's got the room, and probably a place to pop in an exercise video. Ask a co-worker to join you.

Bring a Jump Rope

Keep a jump rope in your desk, and go outside to the parking lot for an aerobic workout.

POWER SUITS

The corporate look that brought women to the forefront of the workplace is no longer necessary, and is becoming cliché. Start breaking up every suit in your closet. Remove excess padding from jackets. Try putting those jackets with simple dresses. Alternate tailored shirts with T-shirts and shells.

LOOK PRETTY IN PINK

You can wear pastels in the office and still look efficient and polished. Use softer colors as accents. A pastel sweater set looks chic, yet feminine. Stay away from anything that's too fussy or too floral.

OFFICE MAKEUP

The trick of making up for the office is to look natural under those fluorescent lights, and to keep your makeup on all day.

PREPARE YOUR FACE FOR THE DAY

Before you put on your makeup, splash your face with cool water. Makeup adheres best to cool skin. Pat dry.

Use an oil-free lotion to allow foundation to go over smoothly.

HINT: Use a cotton ball since the oil on your fingers can add to shine.

CREATE AN UNBUDGEABLE BASE

Use an oil-free foundation. Cream-to-powder foundations work well because of their consistency. If you sponge on the base it will adhere better.

Press loose powder into your skin to set the foundation.

LONG-LASTING EYE COLOR

1. Fill in brows with a brow powder, and then brush over with a toothbrush sprayed with hairspray or gel.

2. Use a neutral eye shadow and sweep the color over the entire eyelid. Use a brush so that the color will not appear too cakey.

3. Line the eye with eye pencil, then seal it in with a coordinating eye shadow brushed over it.

4. Curl lashes, then apply two coats of waterproof mascara.

LIPS THAT STICK

1. Line lips with a neutral colored lip liner. Outline outside the lip with a brush dipped in concealer. It will keep color from smearing or feathering all day.

2. Apply lipstick with a lip brush. Blot, then holding a tissue over lips, powder over.

HAIR HOLDERS

More and more working women are finding hair accessories to be a more attractive alternative to just putting their hair up in a traditional bun.

 HINT: A small butterfly clip is fine, but save the rhinestone accessories for after hours.

Don't even think about wearing those big jaw clips in your hair. I don't even think they should be worn out of the house.

OFFICE TO EVENING

There are times when we don't have time to go home and change into party clothes. That's why it's so important to plan a working wardrobe that will be able to segue into nighttime activities.

CLOTHING CHANGES

• Wear a camisole under your closed suit during the day. Make certain that even with the jacket closed, you are not showing cleavage.
• Bring rhinestone jewelry and strappy heels with you to work.
• Change into a sequined T-shirt.

• Add a satin shirt to a basic pair of trousers.
• Change hosiery from opaque to sheer.
• Change to a smaller purse. Always keep a small purse inside your business bag.

QUICK MAKEUP CHANGES

• Intensify lip color and eye color.

• Add shimmer and glitter.
• Apply gloss over lip color and eye color.
• Blot off excess oil with a tissue and re-powder.

SPEEDY HAIR CHANGES

• Turn hair upside down and brush through.
• Spritz hair through the roots.

• Turn hair back up and adhere a soda can on top of your head with an elastic band or a ponytail at the crown. Keep it in for at least thirty minutes before heading out. You may want to do this late in the day after everyone's gone.

Chapter 11

SPECIAL OCCASIONS

STEP OUT IN STYLE

Whether you're heading out to that annual event or entertaining at home, half the fun is how you'll look. Go bolder and brighter with your clothing, makeup, and accessories. Do something different with your hair.

DRESS CODES

Casual/Informal

You'll never go wrong with a classic trouser and blouse. Stay with a low heel. Accessories should be minimal.

Cocktail

If the event is after work, wear your daytime suit with some changes. Add more makeup and a beaded bag.

A basic black dress is perfect with a jacket. Because cocktail parties can run the full range, you can always remove the jacket. Doing so will create a dressier look.

Semiformal

The black dress works with rhinestone or crystal jewelry. A safe bet for many women is an elegant evening suit. Dressy heels and jewelry complete this look.

Formal

Although a long dress is no longer required, it would be appropriate if that is the look you find comfortable. Mid-calf or knee length is fine if the dress has elaborate detailing.

Black Tie

Think understated formal. A long dress is appropriate as well as a shapely dress with fancy jewelry.

SEASONAL PARTY WEAR
When It's Cold Outside

A little velvet is always in good taste, and will add instant sophistication to what you already have in your wardrobe.

Dress it up with:

Lace or sheer blouse

Faux gems

Glittery tops light up any party with their interesting textures and yarns. For a casual party, team it with wool. To take it to the max for a gala event, add shimmery hose.

HINT: Know when enough is enough in glitter and shimmer. You don't want to look like a walking Christmas tree.

Also consider:

an iridescent blouse

a charmeuse tunic

a fluffy angora sweater

When the Weather Heats Up

In the warmer months, the look of lots of skin is what works if the body is right for it. The look for those heated nights is all about brightness and movement. Anything too elaborate or weighty won't work.

The Look

Bare shoulders

Sheer fabrics

Light floral prints

THE ULTIMATE EVENING BAG

Carry as little as possible in the smallest, sassiest bag you can find.

Absolute Essentials

Just enough cash

Lipstick (it doubles as blush and can smooth out eye shadow)

Compact with mirror

Breath mints

Comb or foldable brush

If There's Room

Cell phone

Key

Credit card

Hanky

Mascara

Eye pencil

Super Glue (to tack back false eye lashes and reattach a false nail)

EVENING BAG ALTERNATIVES

Cosmetic bag

Designer handbag cases

Child's purse

Jewelry pouches

PUTTING ON A PARTY FACE
Not Your Daytime Face

Your regular makeup routine just won't work at night. You need to double the intensity of your cosmetics, otherwise, your makeup won't show up at all in the dark. Go for a brighter blush, darker lipstick, etc.

Lip Gloss

Use it over your regular lipstick. It will give your lips a sultry look and catches the light.

Luminescence

Shimmery powder dresses up your face. A matte look is not appropriate for nighttime lighting, and it can cause your face to look older. Use cream or stick luminscent highlighters to enhance cheeks, lips, and brow bones.

Choose One Feature

Select one feature on your face to focus on when applying makeup. Dark eyes and light lips direct from the sixties is brought to the present by glossing over lips. This look blends drama with innocence. Still popular is the dark, lined lip. Further the focus by wearing jeweled earrings. The light from the earrings will bring attention immediately to the lips. It's like a neon sign.

Black Eye Shadow

There's only one evening eye shadow color you need, and that color is black or a very close companion like navy, or burgundy. These are colors that would never be worn in the daytime except on the runway, but at night they will intensify your lighter eye shadows.

1. Use it on the outer corner to widen the eye. Take a small brush and create a sideways "v", extending slightly outside the eye.

2. With a pointed brush, line under lower lashes for a dramatic smoky look.

Night Lips

Add gold or silver shadow to the middle of the lip. Blend slightly to make it appear translucent.

Blush

A pop of color on the cheeks gives a glow, which would appear too garish during daylight hours.

FASHION COUNTDOWN

The switch from day to night doesn't have to take an afternoon. Once you're dressed for the day, a few additions to your makeup will have you ready in minutes.

GET READY IN LESS THAN THIRTY MINUTES

1. Start with Your Hair

Just a few rollers will add height, volume, and a little extra shape. Spritz gel or hairspray before rolling.

2. Highlight

Add white shadow to the inner corners of the eye and on browbone.

Highlight just above cheekbones with the same shadow.

3. Line Lips

Pencil all over remaining lipstick with a deep lip pencil. Smooth gloss over entire lip.

4. Touch Up

Using a concealer stick, go over under eye area, around mouth, and anywhere else that could use more coverage.

5. Final Touch

Using a large brush, go over entire face. Apply in a circular motion.

FIFTEEN MINUTES OR LESS

1. If hair is long, pull it in a pony tail at the crown.

2. Slick hair back with a glittery spray.

3. Line eyes with a glittery pencil. Eye shadow is too time-consuming.

4. Apply shimmery powder.

5. Revive lip color with a coat of gloss.

6. If hair is curly, roll front section back and secure with bobby pins to create romantic ringlets.

THE LOOK

MAKING UP FOR CANDLELIGHT

This is the sexiest lighting around, and requires romantic makeup.

1. Use a light pink eye shadow on the inner corner of the eye.

2. Use pink shimmer cream on cheekbones and on the tip of the nose. These features are "lit" by candlelight.

3. Dab shimmer cream slightly beyond the lip line for a sexy, pouty effect. Dot pink gloss on the center of the lips.

A ROMANTIC EVENING

Think "touchable" when making up for that special date or anniversary celebration.

• Choose translucent makeup. Men hate a face that's obvious. Use a cream-to-powder foundation. This will allow for complete control of the coverage.

• Use a very light styling product in your hair. Consider using only perfume for styling. It contains alcohol and will provide just a hint of hold.

• Wear a light lipstick or gloss.

MODEL'S TRICK: Apply gloss to lip and pencil over it with a neutral-colored pencil. It will give a slight definition of color and shape and will not come off.

• Wear something that makes you feel sexy, even if it won't be seen. Sexy underwear is called for here.

• Get a pedicure because it will automatically put you in a feminine frame of mind.

KEEP MAKEUP LASTING ALL NIGHT

Spray a brush or powder puff with hairspray before dipping into powder.

EVENING HAIR

Put hair in a ponytail high at the crown. Then just before going out, take it out, and brush hair while bent over at the waist. You'll be amazed at the volume.

FRAGRANCE

It's an immediate way of feeling dressed up. Night scents are deeper and more sensual. Scents that work especially well at night are Shalimar, Opium, and Coco.

HINT: If you're wearing a dress that is cut low, don't forget to dab a bit of perfume at the décolleté.

JEWELRY

Always include jewelry when heading out for the evening. It catches the light as you move.

Brunettes look best in white gold and silver.

Blonde complexions are flattered by gold.

Drop earrings

• Only when hair is pulled back.

• Not for short necks.

Studs

• Look great on everyone.

• Diamond studs are everyone's favorite.

UNDERGARMENTS

Panty hose

Choose the strength of control according to your shape and the type of garment you're wearing.

Don't wear panties with hose. It will ruin a smooth line. If you prefer not to wear any hose, then a thong is a must.

HINT: Get a longer length of hose than you need and tuck it under your bra. It will eliminate a line at the waist.

Don't wear reinforced toes when wearing sandals. Nothing looks worse. If you don't want to ruin a smooth line but also don't like the look of hose with sandals, then cut the hose off where the dress hem or slit ends.

Bra

There is a bra for every style. If you can't find one to go under your garment, then try going braless.

HINT: Models often will wrap tape under each breast to hold them up.

SPECIAL EVENTS are a time to socialize. Wearing your hair off your face will help you to communicate better. It also gives a more polished look.

Chapter 12

WONDERFUL WEDDINGS

THE BRIDE

THE PERFECT DAY OF BEAUTY

The beauty goal for every bride is to look beautiful, yes, but more important is to appear relaxed and natural. Don't go for a dramatic change in your look. You want to look like yourself, but at your best. Plus, with all that hugging and kissing, the more makeup you put on, the more will rub off.

PREPARE AHEAD

Since you won't be able to cry about it on the day of your wedding, plan now so there won't be any surprises.

1. Find a salon far enough in advance to take some trial runs. Road test both hair and makeup with all the accessories, including the veil. Not only do you want to ensure that you have the right lipstick color, but you want to make sure that you don't have any allergic reactions to a new brand of makeup or hairspray.

2. Hold a swatch up to your face in the light in which you'll be seen.

3. Purchase your own cosmetics if you're having your makeup done professionally. You'll want to have them on hand for touch ups, especially your lipstick.

4. Make the appointment on the big day with enough "down" time. You need to consider that something could go wrong that will need to be fixed, or things could just take a little longer. You don't want to spend five hours at a salon, and have to race to the church.

5. Even if you don't normally wear any makeup, the minimum you'll need is mascara, blush, and

lipstick. White has a tendency to wash out the face.

6. Whether you wear your hair up or down, be sure it doesn't hide your face. You don't want it in the way during photos, kissing, and eating.

7. Use as much waterproof makeup as possible. It's least likely to melt off during those long hours.

THREE-DAY COUNTDOWN TO LOOKING YOUR BEST

Three Days Before

Cut out alcohol, which can puff up the face and body.

Stay away from salt and carbonated beverages.

Drink eight to ten glasses of water.

Get your hair colored.

Get your body and eyebrows waxed.

Two Days Before

Get a manicure and pedicure.

Stop using Retin A or any other strong face treatment.

Drink lots of water.

The Day Before

Try to exercise, since you won't have a chance tomorrow.

Take a long, leisurely bath.

Get a good night's sleep.

FINDING THE GOWN

Brides have so many options today. Here's your chance to express yourself with color and with style. Once not an option, color is now the highest form of sophistication. Brides will no longer be dictated to, and designers are well aware of this. Brides today are older (average age thirty to forty-five) and with enough self-sufficiency not to be swayed by overzealous relatives.

Fabrics

Wedding gowns are no longer being made in the intricate heavy fabrics that we've seen in the past. Thank the designer gods. My gown was so heavy that I fainted at my wedding. The relatives are still talking about it twenty-something years later. Beading and lace are still very important details, but it's more unusual and delicate.

Styling

There's a sexy young feeling that's become popular, and even strapless dresses are sought after by today's bride. An interesting back is a nice way to walk down the aisle. Simple drama is achieved with thought-out details.

BUDGETING YOUR GOWN

Of course, you want to get the loveliest dress you can find, but you don't want it to overcome other considerations in your wedding plans.

• Find the style that best suits you. It will narrow your choices and simplify your search.

• Go everywhere and try on everything. Don't feel that your gown needs to come from the most expensive boutique. Consignment shops are a hidden treasure of bridal gowns.

• If it's a great buy, don't worry about the size. With the right adjustments you can have a wonderful gown.

• Check classified ads. There are incredible deals there, and most often, the gowns have been cleaned. You may find an unworn gown, as my friend did as the result of an unfortunate story.

ACCESSORIES

Finding the Right Shoe

The worst thing that can happen to a bride is to wear shoes that hurt. The wrong shoes will even show up on the face. Comfort, color, fabric, design, and heel size are all important considerations.

• Shop for shoes late in the day when feet have swollen and are at their largest.

• The design of the shoe should complement the design of the gown.

• Plan to break in your shoes by wearing them around the house several times before the wedding.

• To prevent slipping, sandpaper the soles of the shoes.

• Even if you're wearing white, the color of the shoe should exactly match the color of the gown. People will notice.

Jewelry

Keep your jewelry to a minimum. Your gown should be the centerpiece. Some brides may choose to wear a tiara, while others may feel complete with the perfect pair of studs. Whatever you choose as the finishing touch to your total look, make each piece count.

• Hairpins and barrettes add charming sparkle.

• A strong bracelet can take the place of gloves.

• Antique jewelry inspires the look of romance.

YOUR MOM'S WEDDING DRESS

It's the ultimate sticky situation. Your mother has been saving her wedding dress lovingly for all these years, waiting for the day you'll walk down the aisle in it. Before you hurt her feelings, try it on. With the right shoes and jewelry, and with a few tailoring adjustments, it may be perfect. And if it doesn't look that great, she's your mother, and wants you to look your best.

Consider taking part of your mother's gown and having it customized to your new gown. It could be anything from unique sleeves to the entire bodice. Perhaps you could add her buttons to your gown. It's something to think about as a peace-keeper.

THE SECOND TIME AROUND

The first and most important rule that everyone seems to agree on, is that it's not appropriate to wear white.

Other guidelines for second-timers

• Wear off-white or any other pastel.

• Don't wear an elaborate gown.

• Consider a dress that's age-appropriate.

• Match your attire to the wedding's setting. If it's an afternoon country wedding it should reflect that. If it's a black-tie event in the evening, a sophisticated touch of glamour is necessary.

YOUR BEST PICTURE EVER

These pictures will be seen for many years. Be certain yours will be ones that will make you proud.

• Use lots of powder. Most cameras (especially flash) will make you look shiny.

• Apply concealer under your brows to make your eyes look bigger.

• Avoid dark lipstick if you're doing any black and white photos. It comes out looking black.

• Don't forget to make your eyebrows a little darker, since they tend to fade out in photos.

• Use shimmer in only one or two areas. It reflects light, and is exaggerated in photographs.

THE WEDDING PARTY

BE KIND TO YOUR FRIENDS

If you've ever been a bridesmaid, you'll be the first to allow your bridal party to help choose the dresses. You, of course, should pick the color scheme, but let your attendants choose a dress that flatters both their figures and finances.

HOW TO PLEASE EVERYONE

Since each of your attendants will most likely have a different figure type, consider choosing different but similar styles in the same color. It will make your wedding line unique and your wedding attendants extremely grateful.

HINT: There are several designers now offering designs for attendants as separates. This allows for the accommodation of all figure types.

GUEST ATTIRE

PANTS

A pantsuit is a chic alternative if worn in a dressy fabric.

BLACK

The old superstition of not wearing black to a wedding because it's bad luck is long past. But do consider navy as a more modern alternative.

WHITE

Don't wear it to a first wedding. It's fine to wear to a second wedding, but I still believe beige shows more respect.

SEQUINS

It's only acceptable if the wedding starts after 6 P.M.

Chapter 13

PREGNANCY CHALLENGES

WHAT TO WEAR

DRESS LIKE A GROWN-UP

Just because you're having a baby, it doesn't mean you have to dress like one. Although most maternity outfits are made to look like oversized baby outfits, you don't have to wear them.

EXTEND YOUR PRESENT WARDROBE

During the first few months of your pregnancy you can get away with wearing your regular wardrobe if you use the old rubber band trick on your pants.

1. Loop one end of the elastic around the pant's button.

2. Thread the other end through the button hole and then back on the button.

3. Use larger elastics as your tummy grows.

START WITH STRETCH

Choose knits in larger sizes. They will expand as you do, and retain their shape after washing.

DON'T BUY TOO MUCH

Maternity clothes are very expensive, and not worth their short life span. The one exception is leggings. They are unbelievably comfortable, and you'll wear them throughout your pregnancy. Buy two pairs, and you're all set.

BORROW FROM YOUR MAN

Use his oversized cotton shirts and sweaters. They go perfectly with leggings. Tell him it's the least he can do for you.

STAY BASIC

Go for solid, neutral colors. They will carry you further, and are most slimming. Pare down as many details as possible. Ruffles, bows, lace, etc., bring unwanted attention to an expanding form. This is the time that tries even the most confident woman's self-esteem. The last thing you need is some ridiculous design that encourages people to pat you on the head.

WORKING YOUR PREGNANCY

If you work, you're going to need to invest in at least one suit with coordinating skirt, pants, and dress. It will make you more comfortable to wear something comfortable and professional looking. Choose a light-weight wool, because most likely you'll need to go through more than one season. Wool also holds up better than other fabrics.

DON'T BE AFRAID TO SHOW OFF

Anything that hasn't been affected by pregnancy should be accentuated. If your legs are great, wear short dresses. If you've prided yourself on your toned arms, then go sleeveless.

STAY CLEAR OF PRINTS

Fashionable florals, polka dots, and other large patterns make the slimmest woman look larger, so why would anyone who is pregnant want any part of it?

KEEP ACCESSORIES TO A MINIMUM

Pregnant women have a difficult time wearing ropes of necklaces or big, dangling earrings. An armful of bracelets will fall right at the belly line and create a sign towards it.

MATERNITY ALL STARS

Drawstring pants

Twinsets

Flowing tunics

TO COLOR OR NOT TO COLOR?

HAIR-COLORING DILEMMA

Pregnant women who color their hair worry that it could cause harm to the fetus.

• Highlighting doesn't touch the scalp and the chemicals are contained in foil, so it is considered safe by the American College of Obstetricians and Gynecologists.

• Single-process treatments can be done successfully using henna, which is ammonia and peroxide-free and lasts four to six weeks.

• Some salons feature vegetable-based, chemical-free hair products. Call around and you're sure to find one.

Use color-enhancing shampoos and conditioners to extend the life of your color.

YOUR BODY AFTER THE BABY

STRETCH MARKS

You can prevent unsightly stretch marks while pregnant.

• Try to keep your weight stable since stretch marks appear when the skin can't adjust to the weight gain.

• Keep your skin moist and supple. Break open a vitamin E capsule and a vitamin A capsule and mix both with a teaspoon of vegetable shortening. Massage it all over the tummy area at night. Try to make it a nightly ritual.

• Take vitamin K as a supplement, or if your doctor doesn't feel comfortable with supplements, add it to your moisturizer. Use it in the morning, or alternate it with the above treatment.

HEALING STRETCH MARKS

There is a new treatment that is available over the counter called Regenetrol that flattens out the ridges of stretch marks. So if a few stretch marks have popped up, give it a try.

RECOVERING YOUR BODY

After delivery, don't be too hard on yourself in getting your body back. Poor body image only exacerbates postpartum depression. Your body won't look like it did before pregnancy. Even when delivery is free of complication, it takes at least six months for the body to recover.

GETTING RID OF UNSIGHTLY VEINS

Horsetail extract is an over-the-counter herb that has the ability to eliminate visible veins. Discuss this with your doctor if you are nursing.

Chapter 14

SEASONAL BEAUTY

SPRING

SPRING CLEAN YOUR SKIN

The extreme temperature fluctuation of winter calls for drastic rescue measures.

Fight the Flakes

Start using an alpha hydroxy regime both in the morning and evening to eliminate dried out winter skin and expose newer, fresher skin.

Mix ¼ cup cornmeal with enough witch hazel to make a paste. Use a small brush (a toothbrush is ideal) and massage mixture into damp skin. Rinse with warm water and pat dry.

CHAPPED LIPS

Gently massage a mixture of ½ teaspoon baking soda and the contents of a vitamin E capsule into lips. Use an old toothbrush or coarse wash cloth. Finish by sealing in with the contents of a vitamin A capsule. Be sure to pat outside of the lips too.

SOFTEN HANDS

Combine one teaspoon glycerin (available at drugstores) with one cup warm mashed potatoes. Dip hands in and relax in this mixture for ten to fifteen minutes. Rinse off and dry. Finish by massaging in a rich moisturizer or petroleum jelly.

EVEN OUT BLOTCHINESS

Winds and harsh temperatures cause skin to crack, irritating lower layers and creating a blotchy complexion. Cure it by applying a hydroquinone cream on areas. These are also known as bleaching creams.

Massage directly into blotchy areas with a paste made of boric acid powder and lemon. Let it remain on blotchiness for a few minutes before rinsing off.

DRY PATCHES

After winter, you are more than likely to find extremely dry patches of skin. Legs are at their worst, catching on hose and feeling itchy. Heavy moisturizing is called for. Solid vegetable shortening is by far the best treatment I've seen. If there was anything more glamorous that worked as well, I'd be first in line. Hospitals use this treatment for psoriasis and eczema, so it should cure winter roughness.

Use a loofah all over your body to encourage exfoliation. A vegetable brush will also work. Winter skin is delicate, so be careful not to rub too hard.

BODY-REVEALING SCRUB

Mix one cup coconut milk with one packet raw sugar and ¼ cup olive oil. Massage into skin and shower off.

GET FEET READY FOR SANDALS

To soften feet, cover them in whole fat yogurt then put on socks. Wear them at least an hour and then soak off the yogurt in warm water steeped in a couple of chamomile tea bags.

Pumice off rough skin and apply a rich moisturizer.

TRANSITION INTO A SPRING WARDROBE

Going into a new season is never fun when it comes to dressing. One day it's raining, the next day it's warm, then the slush comes in. What a mess.

• Change from opaque tights to sheer hose.

• Trade in a leather bag for fabric.

• Add pale colors to accent.

• Switch to shorter lengths.

• Put away your winter coat and bring out the classic trench.

LIGHTEN YOUR MAKEUP

• Switch from dark matte lipsticks to softer, glossy shades. Add petroleum jelly to your current colors for a stained lip.

• Change from powder eye shadows to cream to powder shadows. Oils in powder shadow tend to cake when the weather warms up.

• Go from heavy powder to baby cornstarch. It's a great secret of makeup artists who pride themselves on creating a natural, dewy look without shine.

SUMMER

SUN SMARTS

• Lips, ears, and nose are the first to burn. Apply extra sunscreen here.

• The back of the hand is prone to skin cancer. Use a hand cream with sunscreen.

• Protect part in hair line. Sunscreen may be too runny, so run a lip balm along the part. Most lip balms have a high SPF.

LAST YEAR'S SUNSCREEN

Most sunscreens will last two years. Check for signs of chemical breakdown such as separation, discoloration, and odor changes.

SWEET FEET

Steep a bag of spearmint tea in a basin filled with warm water. Soak feet for fifteen minutes. Spray deodorant on soles and in between toes to keep feet fresh.

• Smooth rough heels by scrubbing them with sea salt. Rub in circular motions with your hands.

TREATING A SUNBURN

• Dip a gauze pad or small wash cloth in a bowl of whole milk. Apply to affected area.

• Combine the contents of vitamin A, vitamin E, and flaxseed oil capsules. Gently pat on sunburned skin.

• Apply aloe vera gel to sunburn. Get an aloe vera plant and keep it in your kitchen for burns of all kinds. Snap off a leaf and gently finger tap on skin.

• Wrap a cup of oatmeal in cheesecloth or the leg from a pair of panty hose. Hang it from your faucet so that the bath water will run over it. Enjoy a soothing bath.

• Take aspirin to bring down swelling.

THE BEST TAN

Use sunless tanning products. Start with a light hand. You can go darker the next day. Apply moisturizer first so that lotion goes on evenly.

◀▶ HINT: Mix baby oil with bronzing powder and smooth on for a tanned look that has sheen and luminescence.

THE SUMMER FACE

During the hardest months of the year for keeping makeup on, rely on pencils. They will stay on for a long time and won't melt. Plus, they'll tuck into a purse or beach bag. Use pencils to line eyes, as a stay-on-forever lipstick, and as blush.

There are wonderful pencils to do all three jobs in every price range available.

SUMMER MAKEUP IS CLEAN AND SIMPLE.

1. Use foundation sparingly and only in places you need it, like the T zone and under the eye.
2. Substitute a moisturizing sunscreen for your regular moisturizer.
3. Bronzing powder is a natural way to give a little definition to eyes, cheeks, and lips.

SUMMER HAIR TIP

For hair that gets too brassy, use silver hair-enhancing shampoo.

SUMMER DRESSING

Start with Basics

Classic shapes work best in warmer weather.

Mix White and Black

Black is forever slimming.

White reflects light and heat and goes with anything.

Stay Simple

Forget excessive jewelry and scarves.

The only accessory you really need is a hat.

Mix Day with Evening

A simple sun dress works both night and day.

Sparkle dresses everything up.

SWIMSUIT SHOPPING

Come on, it's not fun but you've got to do it. Here's how to choose the best suit for your body.

Heavy Thighs

Draw color to the top of the suit and keep the dark color at the hip.

Small Chest

Look for a suit with underwire lift and padding. Don't go up more than one cup size or it will look fake.

Large Chest

Color interest should be on the bottom of the suit, and the top should have an underwire.

Droopy Bottom

Look for a suit that has a spandex or lycra blend and full-seat coverage. These fabrics lift and hug the body.

Thick Waist

Choose a suit with dark colors on the sides and brighter colors in the middle. High-waisted two-piece suits work well to define the waist.

Short Legs

A high-cut suit will make your legs look longer and slimmer.

Darker bottoms and bottoms with banding also provide a leg-lengthening illusion.

Tummy Bulge

Many suits have built-in tummy panels that act like a girdle without the constriction.

High-waisted two-piece suits sometimes have this feature.

FOR A PERFECT FIT

Go up a size so you can move comfortably. A suit that's too snug will cut into you and create bulges.

Look at tags for feature indications. Some suits are designated as slimmers or minimizers.

Check for adjustable and removable straps. You don't want to have lines on your skin.

FALL

FIXING SUMMER'S DAMAGE

Fried Hair

The sun does so much damage to hair (especially the ends), that the only thing you can do is to have a good trim at your salon. Do it now so that it will grow before those holiday parties.

Scorched Skin

Tender loving care is called for here. No matter how diligent you thought you were, there's bound to be damage. Step up to a richer moisturizer, enriched with the contents of a vitamin A capsule to start skin repair.

MAKEUP CHANGES

• Darken summer lipstick by going over entire lip with a slightly deeper pencil.

• Start to use a heavier foundation to even out blotchiness.

• Finish off with a light powder. Oily faces belong to summer.

WARDROBE RENOVATIONS

• Change hose to a darker tone to coordinate or match shoes.

• Get a great jacket that will take you through those chillier days that require more than a T-shirt.

• Pick out a great leather bag to replace summer's fabric or straw tote.

KEEP THAT BRONZE GLOW

Extend the active, healthy look of the outdoors by investing in both a revitalizing lotion (like Ultima's Glowtion) and bronzing powder.

Don't pay a lot because many of the top makeup artists prefer to use drugstore brands such as Wet and Wild's Bronzer or Bonne Bell's Bronzing Powder.

WINTER

Extreme temperatures, blustery winds, and low humidity are reasons we must put our bodies into defense mode for several months.

LESS WATER/LESS SOAP

When the weather turns cold, it seems comforting to warm up in a hot bath or shower. This dries out skin, so it's important to use tepid water, stay in a shorter time, and stop using strong soaps.

Use bubble baths sparingly. They contain detergents that can dry out skin. When cold weather hits, switch to bath oils.

MOISTURIZE MORE

Apply your moisturizer before stepping into the bath so that the steam will accelerate the benefits. Honey is a great humectant to use once a week as a mask.

PROTECT SKIN FROM THE ELEMENTS

Even if you spend most of your time indoors, the drying effects of winter are a real challenge.

• Use gentle exfoliants, especially on chapped areas.

• If using acne medication, protect skin when outdoors by using thicker moisturizer and foundation. A light layer of petroleum jelly will act as a protective layer over moisturizer.

• Stay away from deodorant soaps. They strip away necessary oils.

• Use a humidifier to moisturize drying indoor air.

Three Reasons to Convert to Solid Vegetable Shortening During Cold Weather

1. It readily absorbs into extremely dry, flaky skin.

2. It doesn't contain any irritating additives.

3. It's the cheapest moisturizer you'll ever buy.

STOP WINTER STATIC

Rub fabric softener sheets over hair and inside hats.

Use a leave-in conditioner to add moisture to hair and to flatten cuticle. This makes hair smooth and less prone to static.

Spray Static Guard on your brush or enmesh it with a fabric softener sheet.

Rub a light-hold hair gel into scalp with head bent over.

HANDS

Next to your face, your hands are the part of your body most exposed to environmental damage. Each time you moisturize your face, also be sure to moisturize your hands.

Once a week, sleep with bag balm (available at drugstores) slathered on hands, covered by cotton gloves. Bag Balm (also called udder balm) is a rich salve that was originally created to treat cow's chapped udders.

Paraffin Wax Hand Treatment

Melt paraffin wax in a microwave (find it at supermarkets and hardware stores). Use one bar per treatment. Dip hand in and let harden. Remove and rinse.

Do this once a week and you'll see a great improvement in your hand's texture. This is a well-known, pricey spa treatment that is a cinch to replicate at home.

FEET

Friction from heavy footwear can cause skin to thicken and harden. Use alpha hydroxy moisturizers and always moisturize before putting on socks or hose. This will prevent snags and runs, and allows the natural heat of heavier footwear to accelerate penetration of the moisturizer.

At least once a week, apply a rich moisturizer and sleep in a pair of socks. Sand off rough areas with a block of fine grade sandpaper or foot file.

HINT: I found a terrific moisturizer when I was making an appearance on QVC. I really liked the heavy beeswax consistency. It's called Surgeon's Skin Secret, and it works wonders on feet! Order it from QVC at (800) 345-1515.

HAIR

Limit blow-drying time by blotting moisture with a thick towel.

Always use a heat-protecting style spray.

Use a deep-penetrating treatment that contains oils and proteins weekly.

Use shine-enhancing products. The lack of sunshine leaves hair dull and lifeless. Blondes should consider getting their hair highlighted since the sun is not able to do its warm weather job of producing highlights and contrasting tones.

HINT: Consider getting your hair colored. It coats the shaft of the hair, leaving it fuller and thicker.

Recipe for Flaky Scalp and Dandruff

Add ten drops of tea tree oil to one ounce of shampoo. Massage vigorously into scalp. Use once or twice a week.

LEGS

Since legs have few oil glands, they are prone to extra dryness and flakiness. There is even a flaky condition called "Panty Hose Dandruff." Eliminate it by always moisturizing before putting on hose.

STAYING WARM

• Layer your clothing. It warms the body more efficiently while protecting skin from the drying effects of extreme temperatures.

• Cover your head. Most heat is lost through the top of the head.

• Invest in cashmere. It has more insulating power than any other fabric.

BOOTS

The right boot style can slim legs, add height, and add life to an otherwise dull outfit.

Ankle Boots

Best if you have thicker ankles.

Wear with pants or a long skirt.

Knee-High Boots

These looks best on slim legs.

Wear with short skirts or skirts that fall below the knee.

Mid-Calf Boots

A good look for short legs.

Adds panache to leggings and slim pants.

BOOT CARE

Remove salt from boots with vinegar.

Protect boots with butcher's wax (available at hardware stores and supermarkets).

209

Chapter 15

ACCESSORIES

THE FINISHING TOUCH

Show me a woman who has it all together and I'll show you a woman who has learned the proper art of accessorizing. Accessories not only pull an outfit together, but they allow us to express our individuality. It is the least expensive way to extend a basic wardrobe and is the first evidence of fine taste. I consider an accessory as anything that is used to complete a look, which is why I've included everything from handbags to underwear in this chapter.

THE PERFECT HANDBAG

Your handbag is the most important accessory in your wardrobe. It is seen more easily than your shoes because your bag is closer to eye level.

Never buy a handbag that is larger than 10 inches x 13 inches, unless you're purchasing it solely as a travel bag.

It's not necessary to match a handbag to each and every outfit. Who has time to do this? However, there should be some coordination. Purchase a neutral shade or multicolored bag that will go with most of your wardrobe.

Purchase the best handbag you can find. You'll be using it several times a day, so it will take a lot of wear and tear. It needs to be well-made.

Make certain the bag is not heavy before you fill it.

Find one with at least two separate compartments to find things easily.

Take into account your height and weight. If you're top-heavy, the straps should be a little longer so that you won't be carrying your bag next to your breasts. It will bring attention to them, and could make you look like you have three breasts.

Choose straps that are at least two inches wide and adjustable.

Include the Essentials:

Lipstick (it doubles as a blush)

Compact with mirror (choose dual finish)

Notebook and pen

Wallet

Keys

Breath mints

Comb or brush

Neutral eye shadow (doubles as lip powder)

Eye liner (doubles as lip pencil)

Tissues

Nail file

If You Have Room

Mini pill box with supplies

Sewing kit with small scissors

Mascara

Handbag Don'ts

Never carry loose powder in your bag. Don't purchase a bag that doesn't have security closures. I've seen some embarrassing moments when handbag contents have fallen all over airport security ramps.

SHOES

You love them. You collect them. Shoes are an investment that can make even the dullest outfit into something spectacular.

Shoe Style/Fashion Style
Flats

Long flowing skirt

Long or short narrow skirt

Long casual dress

Slim pants

Heels

Above the knee, tailored skirt

Knee-covering straight or A-line skirt

Dressy trousers

Sandals

A flat sandal looks best with casual pants or long casual skirt.

A strappy mid- to high-heel sandal goes perfectly with a nighttime dress.

Shoe Don'ts

Slides or mules that are too short

Cowboy boots with skirts

White shoes, unless you're a nurse

Boots with hose (wear only opaques)

Clunky shoes with short skirts

Ankle boots with short skirts

Ankle straps with mini skirts

Shoe Care

Coat new shoes with a non-silicone spray. Scotch guard works well.

Maintain shoes with a conditioning shoe cream.

Polish shoes and cover scuffs with a spray polish.

Keep your favorite shoes on cedar shoe trees. Cedar absorbs odor.

HINT: Don't wear the same shoes two days in a row. Give your feet and the shoes a day to recover.

The Perfect Fit

Try on shoes at the end of the day.

Never buy a shoe that bulges over the welt of the shoe.

Don't buy a shoe that wrinkles when you flex your foot.

Leave a one-half inch between your longest toe and the end of the toe box.

Don't buy shoes that have to be "broken in."

Hold backs together to check that they are equal height.

Put each shoe down to make sure that they sit flat.

Look at the inside of the heel to check that the shoe's outside rim is straight.

The top stitching should be straight and well-machined. If it's uneven, it's a sign that the shoe is not well-made.

If you can pull the insole away, the manufacturer hasn't used the right adhesive.

Under the insole there should be a small cushion for comfort.

If you run your finger around the innersole and feel bumps, the wrong nail has been used.

Buying Sandals

The simpler the sandal, the more you'll wear it.

If you wear patterns, buy black or beige sandals.

Be sure the straps are well-made, neither too tight nor too flimsy.

Avoid sandals that have straps that cut into a bunion.

Look for built-in arch support. Inner padding is the sign of a well-made sandal.

Toss Those Shoes If:

A stain can't be removed.

There's a hole in the top material.

The shoe has a rubber sole that's broken.

Repair Them If:

A sole can be replaced.

The zipper on a boot is broken.

The stitching has come undone.

HINT: Put rubber soles on the bottom of leather-soled shoes to make them last longer and to prevent slipping.

The Right Athletic Shoe

Walkers

Choose a shoe with extra cushioning in the midsole. Make sure the shoe bends easily between the heel and toe.

Runners

You need padding in the mid sole, elevated heels, and a higher arch for support. Look for a shield at the back to keep your heel in place.

Tennis

Look for lateral support for side to side movement.

Toe caps are necessary.

Thicker soles will extend the life of the shoe.

HINT: Wash your sneakers in the washing machine, but let them dry naturally. A dryer will shrink them.

HOSIERY

The possibilities are endless. Let me simplify your life. Spandex makes panty hose fit better and last longer.

How to Purchase Hosiery

Ultra sheer hose is the most delicate and allows skin tones to show through.

Business Sheer is semi-sheer hose designed for durability.

Opaques are heavier than sheers and more durable.

Tights are the heaviest and most durable.

Support hose has a large amount of spandex in the leg to reduce leg fatigue.

Total support hose has spandex in panty and leg areas.

Control top panty hose has spandex in the panty to act as a soft girdle.

Do...

Wear black opaque stockings to slim your legs.

Match your shoes and hose when you can. This gives a polished look.

Hand-wash your hose in a mild detergent and a teaspoon of salt.

Use reinforced toes when not wearing open-toed shoes.

Stock up on your favorite hose whenever they go on sale.

Throw out snagged hose or wear them only under trousers.

Use only skin-toned hose when wearing bright colors.

Avoid outdated suntan and cinnamon colored hose.

SUNGLASSES

A finishing touch to any woman's wardrobe are a great pair of sunglasses. Choose a frame that complements your facial structure. Look for a style that balances properly on your face and features flexible templates.

Long Narrow Face

Looks best in wrap around, oval frames.

Round Face

Square shapes are most flattering.

Square Face

Choose round frames.

Long Nose

Stay away from aviator styles.

Lenses for Driving

Go for gray- or green-tinted lenses. They block light evenly, and allow you to see true colors.

Sunglasses Sense

• Get shades with UV protection. Look for 95 percent blockage.

• Polarized lenses will cut glare.

FRAGRANCE

It's the perfect accessory that completes an outfit and sets a mood. It can be overwhelming sometimes with all the different fragrances and the confusing mixture of aromas at fragrance counters.

Don't buy a fragrance without trying it out. Most companies have samples that you can take home. If they don't, apply it to your wrist, neck, or crook of your elbow. Walk around for at least thirty minutes before making a decision. Pay attention to how you like the scent right after applying it, and after thirty minutes.

If you need to make a purchase right away, take the sample outside of the store or at least away from the counter. Rub your hands together to create perspiration, then add a few drops on your palm.

If you're planning to try several fragrances, then bring a plastic bag of coffee beans. Sniff the contents between fragrances to neutralize your olfactory senses.

JEWELRY

Skin Jewelry

Is sensual and feminine.

Includes short necklaces, earrings, rings, and bracelets.

Clothing Jewelry

Is usually worn for business.

Includes pins, long pendants, and chain belts.

Is It Real? How to Tell

Diamonds

Look through the back of a cut stone while holding it above newsprint or paper with writing on it. If you can see even small parts of letters, then sorry, your stone is a fake.

Real diamonds completely distort the print, and you would see only the paper.

Pearls

It's the old "tooth" test that works here. Rub a pearl gently across your bottom teeth. If the gem feels mildly abrasive (like the sand from the ocean it came from), then the pearl is real.

Imitation pearls will feel very smooth and slippery.

Wear your pearls often. It makes them hang properly, and contact with the skin keeps them moisturized.

Jewelry at Work

In the office, jewelry can give ordinary work clothes individuality and style. It can offer up fun and sparkle to an otherwise serious environment. Keep jewelry understated, but go for one bold piece.

Bracelets shouldn't get in the way of writing or typing. Dangling bracelets won't work with an office look.

One or two pins with a theme open up conversation and make a statement. Several pins look like a walking jewelry chest.

A little personal style at work makes you sophisticated and noteworthy.

Jewelry Do's

Mix metals. Silver and gold looks contemporary.

Mix pearls with metals. It breaks up that overly feminine look.

Bring a look into the evening with crystal or rhinestones.

Combine a short choker with long strands.

Use a bracelet to create a cuff.

Add jewelry to handbags, lapels, and pockets. Pins can make a daytime purse a nighttime spectacular.

Use pins to break the ice where you're not known.

Use pins as a necklace enhancer to change a look.

Tack down a scarf with a coordinating pin.

Dress up denim.

Soften the look of leather with pearls.

Mix real gems with fake.

Cut down shiny materials with matte.

Wear estate jewelry.

Wear a pin near your shoulder. It will diminish any posture imperfections.

Shop flea markets for great jewelry bargains.

Wear dangling earrings with a turtleneck.

Make a statement with the perfect earring.

Jewelry Don'ts

Wear dangle jewelry at work.

Wear jewelry in your nose or on your tongue.

Wear both a big necklace and big earrings.

Wear a daytime watch with evening attire.

Put a dainty ring on a large hand.

Wear pendants longer than the belt line.

Neglect to coordinate jewelry with your belt.

Forget to clean your jewelry.

BELTS

Chain Belts

Wear a chain belt as jewelry. Loosely draped around the hips, it can take attention away from a larger waist.

Thin Belts

Wear a small belt if you want to provide definition to an outfit without bringing attention to the waist.

Think Monotone

Wearing a belt in the same color as a skirt or trouser will create a slimming look.

SECRETS OF SCARVES

Use a scarf as a **colorful belt.**

A scarf is a chic **head wrap**.

A large scarf around the waist is a **pareo**.

Fill in a suit by using a scarf as an **ascot**.

A small scarf is a fun **wristband**.

A rolled scarf makes a casual **necklace**.

Make any **hat more festive** by adding a scarf.

Chapter 16

GETTING ORGANIZED

THE BIG CLEANUP

To get the most from your wardrobe you've got to establish an organized system. You want to be able to be ready at a moment's notice, looking and feeling totally pulled together.

START IN YOUR CLOSET

1. Go through your closet and pick out anything you haven't worn in over a year.

2. Get rid of mistakes. If it doesn't make you look great, if you're tired of it, if it still has its tags, then give it to charity.

3. If it has a great deal of sentimentality linked to it but you never wear it, then put it in a box, and tuck it under your bed or in the basement. But don't let it take up valuable space in your closet if you don't wear it on a weekly basis.

4. If it doesn't fit and it can't be tailored, toss it. Face reality. It hurts more to look at that garment than it does to clear it out.

5. Make repairs. Chances are, you're not wearing it because it's not ready to go out. If you don't take them to be repaired in one month, then you know you're really not that crazy about it.

Put Clothes into the Following Categories:

1. Looks good and fits.

2. Would look great if it fit.

3. Never looked that great but is almost new.

Keep the first category, think seriously about the second category, and think about consigning the third category. Your mistake could be someone's else's party dress.

TOSS IT OUT NOW, I DON'T CARE HOW GREAT IT FITS!

Anything plaid, especially kilts

Everything flannel, especially shirts and certain nightgowns

Bell bottoms

Logo tee shirts

Nylon warm-up suits

What Stays

1. The first thing to put back in the closet are those out-of-season clothes. Keep them separated to avoid confusion. A garment bag will do the job.

HINT: Cut a small opening in a pillow case and use it as a garment bag.

2. Next to the garment bag, put your special-occasion clothing. If you have several outfits, consider putting them in another garment bag. In the bottom of the bag, store the jewelry, shoes, hose, and other accessories that are used only with this clothing.

3. Right in front of you when you open your closet should be only the clothes you wear all the time.

4. Group together shirts, then pants, then suits, so it's easy to find things fast every morning or when you're rushed for time.

5. You may need to trim out some items. How many black skirts do you really need? Keep the higher quality, better-made items.

AIR OUT YOUR CLOTHING

Install a hook on the outside of the door. Use it to air out the clothing you wore before returning it to the closet. Doing this will save you money on dry cleaning.

USE A FULL-LENGTH MIRROR

Install one on the inside of the closet door, or use a free standing mirror. You need to see your clothing in its entirety to see if an item is really working for you.

YOU NEED LIGHT

It is absolutely necessary to have a bright light installed in your closet. You need to see what you have in order to wear it.

TAKE CARE OF YOUR SHOES

Take your favorite shoes to be re-heeled and resoled.

Get rid of outdated shoes. Nothing can date an outfit faster.

Toss any shoe that is uncomfortable. Realize that over the years, your shoe size has changed. Your foot has gotten bigger or wider, and it's not going to shrink.

Invest in shoe trees or keep shoes in shoe boxes. Stuff shoes with tissue or newspaper to hold their shape. Take a picture of the shoe and staple it on the box so that you won't have to open every box to find your shoes.

ORGANIZE YOUR MAKEUP

1. Dump every cosmetic you own in a big pile on several layers of newspaper. Separate everything by category. Lipsticks should go in one pile, shadows in another, etc.

2. Toss anything you haven't used in six months, even if it's a "gift with purchase" that you've never even used.

3. Get rid of anything that has an odor, is messy, or is running.

4. Dump foundations and any other cosmetic that has separated.

5. If you're holding on to any makeup color that doesn't flatter you, either combine it with something else to create a new color or toss it out.

All Star Makeup Bags
The "Zip Loc" Bag
They're great for travel and save space. You can easily see when something has spilled. They are the No.1 favorite of airline attendants.

TRANSPARENT PENCIL CASE
You'll wonder why you ever paid big bucks on a cosmetic case once you've paid less than $2 for my favorite way to carry makeup. At last, you can see your cosmetics at one glance, rather than digging your hands in and making a mess.

MORE ORGANIZATION TIPS

Store panty hose in clear baggies to prevent runs.

Tie a knot in the leg of panty hose with runs so you'll know immediately that you can only wear them under pants.

Keep hair-styling products, brushes, and tools in a basket.

Stash makeup in a fishing tackle box or carpenter's tool box. They both feature little compartments that are just perfect for separating shadows by color, pencils (use the screwdriver compartment), etc. Drape a lace doily or a silk scarf over it.

An art bin is a bit pricier but will keep you totally organized.

Tack brass screening to an old picture frame and display your jewelry.

Decorate pins and brooches on a cork bulletin board.

Use a hanger to display all your necklaces. This eliminates unnecessary and time-consuming tangling and knotting that occurs in jewelry boxes.

Invest in padded hangers and spray your favorite fragrance on the padding.

Wrap hangers in tissue paper to support heavier clothing.

Keep necklaces and bracelets from getting tangled by cutting a plastic straw to half the length of the jewelry. Slide it through the straw and clasp it.

Chapter 17

CARE & MAINTENANCE

IT'S ONLY REASONABLE

You've paid good money for your clothing, so it makes perfect sense that you want to keep your things in good shape. You'll expand the life cycle of everything you own while saving money by doing it yourself.

BABY YOUR CLOTHES

Carry baby wipes around with you. They come in handy when you spill something, and they get rid of deodorant stains. All the models put them in their bags.

MAKE YOUR OWN PADDED HANGERS

Take your old shoulder pads (the bigger the better) and pin them to wire hangers. Your clothing will hang better and never have that unsightly ridge again.

HINT: If a wooden hanger has a rough edge that catches on clothing, paint it with a few coats of clear nail polish.

SHOE SAVERS

Use an eyeliner pencil to fix shoe scuffs.

Rub a cotton ball doused with nail polish remover over black marks.

Use an old fashioned rubber eraser to remove grime from suede and fabric shoes.

Dampen a sponge in white vinegar and gently blot away salt stains.

Erase dark marks from pale leather by dabbing with nail polish remover.

Blot grease stains with a paper towel, then massage in talcum powder. Brush off with a soft brush.

Apply toothpaste to stains on white and light-colored shoes.

SHOE POLISH

Use fabric softener sheets as an instant shoe polisher.

Take a banana peel and rub it all over your shoes. Buff and dry. The oils will make your shoes shine like new!

Use a thin coat of hair pomade to shine shoes.

SHOE MAINTENANCE

Get your shoes resoled with a rubber bottom and taps. It will strengthen impact points.

Have your shoe cobbler apply heel shields. They're under $4, and will protect your heels from scrapes and marks.

Have your cobbler steam-clean your suede shoes. Spray them with a waterproofer.

Vary the shoes you wear from day to day to give them a chance to bounce back. It also lessens the chances your feet will develop corns and calluses in a particular spot.

PANTY HOSE POINTERS

Putting panty hose in the freezer overnight before wearing them makes them more run-resistant.

Before wearing new panty hose, soak them in a mixture of ½ cup salt and two cups water. Let them sit for about two hours. Then rinse and drip dry. The salt toughens the fibers and protects them from running and snagging.

HINT: Mist hose with hair spray to make it last longer and prevent static.

STAINS

Toothpaste

Just the way it cleans teeth, toothpaste can act as a stain remover. Rub it on the spot, allow it to dry, and then wash as usual.

White Shirt Stains

Stretch the stained pit over an empty cup.

Pour white vinegar through the shirt into the cup.

Repeat three times.

Then wash as usual.

HINT: Treat stains immediately. As the stain oxidizes, it becomes more difficult to remove.

Scorch Marks

If you've accidentally scorched an item while ironing, lay a wet cloth over the spot. Iron over it a few times, and the mark will disappear.

Stain Prevention

Apply hair spray, perfume, and deodorant at least five minutes before dressing to give them time to dry. Chemicals contained in these products can hurt fabrics.

Oil Stains

Treat a grease stain with talcum powder or cornstarch. Sprinkle it on the stain and let it sit for fifteen minutes. Brush off powder and wash.

Coffee Stains

Mix one teaspoon white vinegar and one teaspoon dishwashing detergent. Apply to fabric.

Blood

Rub in full-strength household ammonia. Rinse promptly. Never use on silk or wools.

Butter

Blot with a non-acetone polish remover. Then rinse promptly with cold water.

Lipstick

Wet a baby wipe with vinegar and dab spot.

Grass Stains

Dab with rubbing alcohol and wash.

Ink or Crayon

Place item stain side down and spray with WD-40. Let it sit for several minutes, then turn over and use on stained side. Gently work in dish-washing detergent. Machine wash using a detergent with color-safe bleach.

Gravy

Rinse with equal parts of ammonia and water until stain disappears.

HINT: If you run out of stain remover, rub liquid antibacterial hand soap into the stain just before washing.

Spit On Those Stains

The enzymes in saliva help break down protein-based food stains. Rub in the saliva with a cloth.

Please, I'm begging you to do this in the privacy of your home or a ladies' room.

KEEP CLOTHES LIKE NEW

1. Close the closet door. Some fabrics fade or streak when exposed to light.

2. Don't wash unless necessary. Each time you do, you lessen the fabric's life.

3. Don't store clothing in plastic. Fabrics need to "breathe."

4. Whiten whites by adding ½ cup baking soda to your detergent.

5. Always hang clothing properly. Zip up zippers, button all buttons, etc. If you won't be wearing the item very soon, stuff arms with tissue paper.

LEATHER AND SUEDES

Soften New Leather

Some new leather, especially less expensive brands, needs to be softened. Rub your new

233

garment with wax furniture polish. This is especially important to do with leather trousers. New leather tends to "creak."

Make Suede Last

1. Treat salt stains with vinegar.

2. Let wet suede dry and then raise the nap with a closely tufted pet brush.

SAVE ON DRY CLEANING

Try to find clothing that has been treated with Teflon. It won't make the garment shiny or uncomfortable, and it will cause stains to fall right off.

KNITS

Turn knits that pill easily inside-out before washing.

Remove pills with a pumice stone or scotch tape.

HINT: Scotch tape performs many more jobs, from tacking up a hem line to anchoring a ponytail.

Don't ever hang knits from the shoulders. Fold them or hang them over the bar of a hanger.

SWIMSUIT CARE

After swimming, rinse suit out in cool water.

Wash suit in a gentle detergent. Regular detergents can harm swimsuit fabrics.

Never wash a suit in the washing machine. It will become misshapen.

If you get any creams or oils on your suit, use shampoo to sponge it off.

Be very careful not to get lotions or sunscreens on your suit.

Block dry your suit. Never put it in the dryer.

Dry your suit thoroughly before packing.

HAT HELP

Hold an old hat over a steaming kettle until damp to eliminate ridges. Stuff with newspaper. Overstuff it if you are trying to stretch the hat out.

ACCESSORY AIDS

Clean cosmetic brushes by dipping them in rubbing alcohol.

Wipe off eyeglasses with coffee filters.

Sharpen lip and eye pencils regularly.

Keep makeup out of sunlight. It can degrade preservatives.

JEWELRY

Cleaners

Boil an ammonia-based cleaner with one cup water. Soak gold, silver, and platinum.

Dissolve two denture cleanser tablets in one cup very hot water.

It is safe to soak most jewelry, even pastes, for up to ten minutes.

Softer gems and most costume jewelry should soak for even less time.

Gold and silver can be soaked for thirty minutes.

Brush clean with a small toothbrush. Rinse and wipe dry with a soft cloth.

HINT: Be very careful about using chemical jewelry cleaners and even sonic cleaners. They have been known to ruin soft gems like corals, pearls, and opals.

Apply a thin coat of clear nail hardener to pearl buttons to restore their luster.

Prevent Skin Discoloration

Apply a thin coat of clear nail polish on the metal links and clasps of your jewelry.

Chapter 18

BODY BEAUTIFUL

CREATE YOUR BEST BODY

There's no magic potion that will get you a great body. But there are short cuts and secrets that the celebrities, models, and others whose figures are their fortunes have used for years. Let me tell you, that they like to eat just as much as you do, but they also know how to take it off. These are the secrets that agents, trainers, and those beautiful people themselves pull out to look as good as they do.

DRINK MORE WATER

When you ask a beautiful celebrity their best beauty secret, they'll state emphatically that they drink a lot of water. Well that's very true, but it's not the whole story. To get optimum benefits from water, you need to drink ice water. With ice water, the body needs to use over twenty-five calories just to warm itself to room temperature in order to absorb the water into the system. That means that the theory of negative calories is true. You are actually using more calories than you are taking in. It doesn't work with celery and it's an old wives' tale about grapefruit, but ice water does have negative calorie effects. Try to drink eight to ten glasses a day.

HINT: A little lemon or an orange slice in your water will make it more palatable.

SPICE IT UP

Scientists have discovered that chili, peppers, mustard, ginger, etc., can actually raise the rate at which you burn fat. How? These foods create a thermogenic effect, meaning they help the body to produce "heat," which burns calories.

HINT: Salsa is only ten calories for two giant tablespoons of it. It's a model's favorite snack. But they eliminate the chips. Plus, the hot salsa will make you thirsty, so you'll want to drink that water.

SUPPLEMENTS FOR WEIGHT LOSS

You've heard it a million times. The safest and most effective way to lose weight is to eat less. If it were that easy, everyone would be successful. Well, the good news is that there are supplements and herbs that really do work to provide that extra advantage in weight loss. These supplements and herbs continue to be all the rage, and new research and data emerges on them all the time. I have included some of this information in previous books, but because it is so popular, and because research is updated so rapidly, I have included it here also. As always, even with natural supplements, I recommend you consult your doctor before introducing them into your diet, and be cautious with their use.

Chitosan

This natural fiber is found in lobster shells and acts like a fat magnet when taken fifteen minutes before eating. Researchers report that since it is non-digestible and binds with dietary fat, it quickly passes out of the body along with fat from the meal you've just eaten. A study revealed that people taking Chitosan lost an average of 8 percent of their body weight. The effect is reportedly enhanced when taken with orange or lemon juice before a meal.

Chromium Picolinate

Scientists have discovered that people who lack chromium in their bodies carry extra weight. The supplement chromium picolinate and chromium polynicotate have been around for a few years. It is an essential dietary nutrient which plays an important role in processing fat and carbohydrates. Many users report that it cuts sweet cravings, too. You could use this supplement if your diet lacks in chromium-rich foods. These foods include mushrooms, apples, broccoli, and cheese. The recommended daily allowance is anywhere from 50 to 200 micrograms. Supplements are usually sold in 200 micrograms, or

239

mixed with other products in varying amounts. This product is readily available in drugstores, health food stores, supermarkets, and general merchandisers.

CLA

Conjugated Linoleic Acid (CLA) is a fatty acid marketed under the name Tonalin. Its purpose is to reduce fat by inhibiting the body's ability to store fats. CLA also increases muscle tone, improves food efficiency, and contains antioxidant properties.

Coenzyme Q 10

This is useful for obesity, coronary heart disease, lack of energy, and high cholesterol levels. Studies have found that some overweight people have low levels of coenzyme Q 10 (CoQ10) and by supplementing it, they can help control their body weight. Recommended dose is for up to 90 mg of CoQ10 without side effects. Anyone with heart disease should first check with their doctor.

Creatine

This non-caloric enzyme can create better muscle tone safely and increase endurance for longer workouts. Creatine works by helping the body retain water in the muscle tissue, which helps to heal the muscle more efficiently without bloating the body. Recommended dosage is ten to twenty grams a day for the first week, then five grams a day. Creatine monohydrate is available in capsules, bars, and shakes.

Garcinia Cambogia

Garcinia cambogia is a yellow fruit from Southeast Asia. Used in cooking, the garcinia extract is added to make meals more filling. Said to aid digestion, it contains hydroxyl citric aid, which is similar to the citric acid in citrus fruits.

Research conducted in the 1970s at Brandeis University, and later by Hoffman-LaRoche (the pharmaceutical company) showed that rats fed hydroxyl citrate shed 25 percent of their body fat in twenty two days. The rats lost body fat partly because hydroxyl citric acid inhibits an enzyme that converts surplus carbohydrate calories into fat.

Available in pill form and in bars at health food stores, garcinia cambogia has taken the natural weight loss industry by storm. It controls the appetite in a natural, safe way, and has no side effects. It is unlike any of the chemicals sold as diet pills.

How to take it

This is a supplement that is most effective taken thirty to sixty minutes before meals. Take it with a glass of water, or with a piece of fruit. Taking it with a bowl of soup also seems to help.

Glutamine

This amino acid promotes uptake of nutrients to build muscle tissue.

HMB

The latest fat-burning and muscle-building protein supplement to impress experts is beta-hydroxy-methylbutyrate (HMB). Studies show that taking three grams of this substance daily causes athletes to gain 63 percent more muscle size and strength and lose twice as much fat as those exercisers who didn't take it.

L-Carnitine

This supplement is reported to accelerate the benefits of chromium. Leading fitness buffs and die-hard weight watchers take the two together. It is sold as a separate unit, and in combination with other supplements. L-Carnitine is an amino acid, which may be in short supply in many diets. The recommended dosage for this supplement is from 250 to 500 mg daily.

Meridia

This is a prescription drug that is meant to be safer than its predecessors, fen-phen and Redux. It is prescribed only for people with a body mass index of thirty or above. Owing to the history of problems with other prescription weight loss products, you would be well advised to check that your physician has been properly informed about Meridia.

Orlistat

This new prescription diet drug works directly on the intestine. It is part of a group of drugs called "lipase inhibitors." Lipase is an enzyme in the intestine that breaks down fat. This drug works on that enzyme to prevent the absorption of fat by about 30 percent.

Pregnenolone

This hormone is produced naturally in our bodies, but production decreases after the age of thirty-five. Not only does it contain anti-aging benefits, but it makes it easier for people to lose weight, improve muscle, and improve skin tone. Recommended dosage is 10 mg two or three times a week.

Pyruvate

Found in red apples, and now available in capsules, this natural substance has almost thirty years of research to back up its claims and safety features. Use it to help burn fats and carbohydrates more efficiently.

Sibutramine

A new prescription-only appetite suppressant that works by maintaining high levels of serotonin, the blood chemical that triggers fullness. Those taking it experience fewer cravings and eat less. The exciting results of extensive studies is that it enabled two out of three people to lose 5 to 10 percent of their body fat safely and without additional dieting or exercising.

Vanadyl Sulfate

This nutrient helps build lean muscle tissue by increasing amino-acid uptake.

HERBS THAT HELP SHED POUNDS

There are herbs you can add to your diet as supplements, teas, and foods that will help your weight loss program go smoothly. Some can even be sprinkled into your bath.

Alfalfa

Aids digestion and acts as a diuretic. It belongs to the special vegetable family of nitrogen-fixing legumes.

Aloe Powder

Causes temporary water-weight reduction because of its strong laxative effects.

Aloe Vera

Helps to maintain regularity among its other benefits.

Bladder wrack

Improves thyroid function and is a bulk laxative.

Burdock

Improves fat metabolism and acts as a diuretic.

Capsicum

This will produce heat to rev up the metabolism and burn fat.

Cardamom

Improves circulation and digestion. A thermogenic herb.

Cayenne

Improves circulation and digestion. Has thermogenic effects.

Chickweed

Long reported as a weight loss tool by herbalists, but not widely tested scientifically.

Cinnamon

Creates a thermogenic burn.

Dandelion root

Aids fat metabolism by affecting the liver.

Ephedra (Ma Huang)

Without a doubt, the most controversial herb on the market today. Some have called it "legalized speed." It stimulates the nervous system, suppressing appetite. It also allegedly speeds metabolism. The side effects are dizziness, jitters, insomnia, and heart palpitations. Abusing the dosage has led to stroke, heart attack, and seizures.

Fennel
A diuretic that reduces hunger and improves energy.

Flaxseed
A bulk laxative that helps curb hunger. Flax swells in the stomach and intestines to promote a sense of fullness.

Green tea
Aids fat metabolism and increases energy.

Guarana
Helps to reduce hunger and has a laxative effect. It contains caffeine, and is reported to speed metabolism and burn fat.

Gymnema Tea
Is your problem a sweet tooth? Gymnema tea coats your tongue, tricking it into finding real sugar bland. The effect lasts for two to three hours. Dieters report that it takes away their desire for doughnuts, cakes, cookies, etc.

Hawthorn
Reduces blood fat and improves circulation.

Kava
This distant cousin to black pepper contains ingredients that produce physical and mental relaxation. Especially useful for stress-related eating.

Kelp
This is a sea plant that is available in capsule form. It helps thyroid function, which regulates the metabolism.

Kola nut
A stimulant that decreases appetite and aids in the metabolism of fat.

Papaya

Aids digestion.

Parsley

A diuretic and nutritional aid.

Phyllium

Helps to curb hunger and allow the elimination of wastes from the body.

St. John's Wort

Known as the natural alternative to Prozac, it works to increase the production of the brain chemical serotonin, boosting mood and curbing overeating associated with depression. It's often used in combination with ephedra to battle weight problems, especially eating disorders and binge eating.

Senna

An all-natural laxative. It's found in weight-loss teas to stimulate the colon. Use occasionally. Just like any other laxative, it can become habit-forming.

Spirulina

Also known as blue-green algae, spirulina contains a natural appetite suppressant. It is a rich source of phenylalanine, a naturally occurring substance that helps create a feeling of fullness after eating.

Stevia

A little-known South American herb called Stevia rebaudiana-bertoni has not one calorie, yet is up to 300 times sweeter than sugar. Use it in its powder form to sweeten beverages. It's a natural alternative to aspartame and saccharin.

Valerian Root

If stress sends you right to the refrigerator, this natural tranquilizer will stop you from overeating.

Vinegar

Ancient healers have used vinegar for thousands of years. Take two teaspoons of vinegar mixed with a glass of water at each meal. The vinegar will help your body to burn fat, rather than store it. Use any vinegar that appeals to you. Apple cider vinegar is a delicious flavor to try. Vinegar is a natural storehouse of vitamins and minerals. Experiment and come up with the tastes that you've never before experienced.

FACE YOURSELF

You can purchase a mirror that attaches to the front of the refrigerator. You'll find that if you have to face yourself each time you peek in, it just may wake you up to reality. Since we open the refrigerator on the average of twenty-two times a day, it will come in handy.

Constantly going into that refrigerator can tempt you as much as entering the most delectable ice cream shop or bakery. You need to either clean it out or cover it up.

AN ASPIRIN A DAY WILL BURN FAT AWAY! The key is thermogenesis, the chemical process by which your body generates heat and speeds up your natural metabolism. Aspirin revs up the metabolism, making it run faster, burn hotter, and vaporize fat effortlessly. Less fat in the body can also unclog arteries and slash your risk of heart attacks and strokes by fifty percent. Of course, you should check with your doctor.

THE TEN TOP DIET FOODS

1. Egg Whites

They're made of pure protein and a blend of important amino acids.

2. Sweet Potatoes

Rich in vitamin A, C, and B6.

3. Broccoli

Only twenty-five calories for a three-ounce serving and 155 percent of the recommended daily dosage of vitamin C.

4. Lentils

A great source of plant protein and rich in other nutrients.

5. Whole wheat pasta

Contains more fiber and more nutrients than regular pasta.

6. Carrots

Extremely high in beta carotene and vitamin A.

7. Tuna

Contains omega-3 fatty acids responsible for lowering cholesterol.

8. Oatmeal

Contains linoleic acid, an essential nutrient.

9. Bananas

Loaded with potassium and other valuable nutrients.

10. Turkey

Leaner than any other meat.

FIGHT FAT WITH COFFEE

New studies have revealed that the amount of caffeine found in a cup of coffee can raise your metabolic rate by 4 percent. If you drink it prior to working out, the results are even greater. Caffeine helps mobilize body fat and make it available as fuel for exercising muscles. This has both a fat-burning effect, and makes working out less tiring.

UNFILTERED APPLE CIDER VINEGAR

What a versatile product! It's a great blood purifier when you put a tablespoon in a cup of hot water and drink it. You can also use it as an astringent for both your face and hair. In cold water it detoxifies, burns fat, and acts as an appetite suppressant. Experiment with flavors. Raspberry is also delicious.

MODELS' & CELEBRITIES' CRASH DIETS

Rebecca Romijn cuts out all refined sugar and stops snacking.

Candice Bergen stops eating solid food and switches to cranberry juice mixed with seltzer and watermelon.

Ann-Margret is another actress who turns to watermelon to quickly lose the pounds. She eats it exclusively all day long, but eats a regular dinner.

Carol Alt is a quick weight loss expert as most models are. She crashes by having a yogurt for breakfast, an apple for lunch, and a chef's salad for dinner.

Cheryl Tiegs breakfasts on juice, eggs, and sparkling water. Lunch is chicken and vegetables. Dinner consists of an omelet and fruit.

Jamie Lee Curtis eats cereal for supper to blitz off the weight.

Ivana Trump relies on egg whites when getting in shape quickly.

DINING OUT

Eating in a restaurant can become creative combat in any diet program. However, with these little steps, it can be a pleasant break from a boring routine without costing a lot of calories.

Don't Arrive Famished

Have a few glasses of water with lemon, and a few carrot sticks before heading out.

Save the Alcohol for the Meal

If you enjoy any kind of alcohol when you are dining out, have it during your meal, not before. Alcohol is a high-calorie beverage, and can stimulate your appetite. It can also impair your judgment about food choices. After all, wines especially enhance the enjoyment of the meal.

Leave Out the Bread Basket

Ask that the breads arrive with the meal, otherwise you'll make a meal out its contents. If you're truly hungry, order an appetizer that takes work to eat. A good choice would be steamed clams, escargot, or soup.

Diners are most likely to eat foolishly during the first ten minutes of a social gathering.

Chapter 19

FIGURE FLATTERY

LOOK POUNDS THINNER

Did you know that you can look ten or twenty pounds thinner in only ten or twenty minutes? That's what celebrities do. This is what I have to do when I work with them. Having weight fluctuations is a fact of life. I've gone on countless TV shows to do makeovers, and my most memorable appearances have been my "pounds paring" productions. I'm about to share with you my very best secrets so that when you've gone up on the scale you no longer have to make a public announcement. I know many women who turn down invitations because they don't want anyone to know they've gained weight. This is no way to live, and you never have to be that desperate again.

You'll probably use these tips, thin or not, because we always want to show others our very best.

BRONZING POWDER

Looking to slim down your face with makeup? Head to your local drugstore, and pick up an inexpensive bronzing powder. Use it to slim down your nose by running it down the sides. Create the illusion of cheekbones in a much more subtle and believable way by running the bronzer under the cheekbone area. Disguise a double chin by running the bronzer under the jaw line.

Can't find any bronzing powder? Choose face powder in a color two shades darker than your foundation.

OTHER MAKEUP TIPS

Highlight your chin, forehead, nose bridge, and brow bone

Dust a translucent face powder over the tip of your chin to emphasize its length. Use over the nose to focus the attention on the top, rather than the sides of the nose. Bring attention to outside of the eyes, widen and lift them with powder.

Play Up Your Brows

Bringing attention to your eyebrows will take it away from that double chin, puffy cheeks, etc. The brow is known as the "frame for the face." Darken your brow a bit, eliminate any stray hairs, and be sure to brush upward. Keep your brows in place with a bit of hair spray. Spray it on an old toothbrush (or even on your index finger).

Emphasize Your Eyes

Line the lower rim of your lids with a white pencil. Curl upper lashes with an eyelash curler. Apply at least two coats of mascara to the upper lashes only. Apply shadow only at the outer corners of the eye in the shape of a sideways "v".

Elongate Your Hands

Little tricks you can use on your nails will help your hands look longer and thinner.

Switch to a lighter shade of nail polish. Stay with beige and pink tones, so that they will blend right into your skin.

If your nails are short, lengthen them by applying polish only on the center portion of the nail. Leave a sliver of bare nail on either side.

FAKE A GOOD BODY

Male and female models do it all the time. They work their muscles just before a photo shoot. If you have an event coming up, don't panic! You too can create a temporary "pumped" look. Here are some things you can do just before going out so you can really look good in that body-revealing outfit.

• Holding a ten-pound weight, slowly lift, bending arm at elbow. Slowly lower. Repeat twenty times.

• Holding a ten- or twenty-pound weight behind the head with both hands, slowly lower hands to the middle of the back. Be sure to hold elbows close to the head. Repeat twenty times.

• You CAN wear that backless dress. Lift your arms straight out to the sides and squeeze shoulder blades toward each other. Count to ten and release. Do this at least fifteen times. Holding five- to ten-pound weights will yield optimum results.

• Fake long, sleek legs by raising up on tiptoes for as long as you can. Try to go a full minute. Raise up and down quickly. This will give your calves a firmer, more toned appearance.

• Wear the highest heels you can walk in without killing yourself.

• Hit the shower with a moisturizing exfoliator to slough off dead skin on arms and elbows.

• Shave with a moisturizing cream to avoid nicks.

• Cover blemishes with a good concealer, even on your shoulders and back.

• Fake cleavage by dipping a brush into bronzing powder and dusting a half-moon contour on each breast. Start from above the breastbone, and go over and up to the armpit. Do this very subtly and no one will ever know.

• Apply a self-tanner all over your body.

BEAT THE BLOAT

Use these model's tips to look more svelte in even the most body-revealing clothing.

• Never drink from a straw, and never chew gum. This will send air right to your tummy and distend and bloat you.

• Avoid starches like pasta and bread. These foods cause the body to produce excess insulin, which puffs you out.

• Eliminate salt for at least twelve hours before putting on anything revealing.

• Eat a few bites of protein. Turkey and fish are excellent choices for energy, and they'll keep you bright and wary of the fattening stuff.

• Don't drink soda, not even diet. Doing so will give you a false, "fatter" BMI reading. This is because it puffs up your body temporarily, even though there are no calories. It's the sodium that causes you to retain the fluid responsible for this condition.

• Rush blood to specific body areas for a more defined appearance.

Balancing on your knees on the floor, lift and lower your arms in one controlled movement. Do three sets of ten each.

Lie down with your legs raised in the air, knees slightly bent. Tuck your hands behind your head. Slowly lift your buttocks a few inches off the ground, squeezing them together as you lift. Hold to a count of twenty. Lower slowly. Do this at least twenty-five times.

Hold the back of a chair, legs spread apart, and toes pointed out. Squat until your thighs are parallel with your feet. Do this thirty times.

YOU CAN WEAR SHORTS

They just have to be the right style. Sorry, no "Daisy Dukes" for you if you're not in perfect shape.

Drawstring shorts can make heavy thighs look slimmer, and reduce any waist.

Pleated shorts slim down a puffy tummy and offer a longer line.

Cigarette and capri shorts instantly make your legs look long and lean. Chubby knees look great in the new just-below-the-knee pedal-pusher styles.

Walking shorts with a wide waistband actually raise your waist.

Nothing ruins the look of a streamlined body more than a big, cluttered handbag. Take all the junk out and throw away any bag larger than 10 inches by 13 inches.

GET RID OF THAT BIG HANDBAG

This is especially important for large-breasted women who look top-heavy with an oversized purse.

HELP FOR PEAR SHAPES

Pear-shaped bodies are heavier below the waist, just like the fruit. The way to balance this figure type is to pad on top.

• Look for bosom-maximixing details like epaulets, breast pockets, and large buttons and embellishments.

• Look for Empire styles.

• Layer a shirt or sweater over a tee shirt or turtleneck.

HELP FOR APPLES

This body type (large torso and breasts with thin legs) needs help minimizing the bust line.

• Make sure that the shirt is fitting without gapping. But don't buy too large of a size, an oversized shirt will only cause you to look bulky.

• Choose a long pendant to lengthen the torso.

• A V neck will elongate and slim.

• Choose a top that hits the hipbone. Stay away from tucked-in styles.

LOOKING LEGGY

Legginess is in the eye of the beholder. There are easy ways to fake the look even if legs are not your strong point.

• Wear a front-slit skirt. If you can carry off a long length, it will help even more.

• Match footwear, hose, and skirt.

• Wear opaque hose with short skirts.

• Wear some kind of heel, even with pants. Remember, the more casual the look, the thicker the heel. Flats squish you like a bug.

• Always choose slim pants over flared or palazzo styling.

• Wear long boots if you've got thick calves and ankles.

• Choose a pencil skirt over a full dirndl type.

- Never wear shiny or textured hose.
- Stay away from straps.
- Don't even think about socks, even with pants.

CLOTHES THAT ADD WEIGHT

Pleated skirts

Fabric without substance

Large patterns

Accessories that are too dainty

Teeny tiny handbags

Clingy fabrics

Frilly, silly clothing (stick with classics)

USE BODY-SHAPERS

The right lingerie can slim, tone, and lift you in all the right places. This gives your body a new look before you even begin losing the weight. While you're going down, it can keep loose skin streamlined instantly!

Some Choices:

Power slips

Uplift shapers

Slimming panty hose

Tummy-toning panties

CLOTHING THAT TAKES OFF POUNDS

Color

One color from head to toe streamlines the body.

Scale

A long, sleek jacket over a slim pant or skirt disguises a heavy waist, bust, or rear. A great jacket slims hips and disguises heavy thighs.

Size

Oversized clothing can give you a bulky look. Choose outfits that are tailored, but not confining. An impeccable fit creates a streamlined image.

Pattern

Bold prints can be attractive on small areas of the body. Prints draw attention away from flaws.

Fabric

Most effective are fabrics that drape the body gracefully, and are neither too clingy nor too bulky.

HINT: **Get into the habit, whether sitting or standing, of drawing your stomach muscles toward your spine. You'll look slimmer instantly, and you'll improve your posture.**

PLAY UP YOUR BEST

Slim Hips

Longer shirts with side slits bring attention to the hips.

Small Waist

A wide belt will bring attention to your waist like a neon sign. For optimum definition, choose a contrasting color.

Great Cleavage

Choose clinging knits for day wear. At night, drop the neckline and add jewelry at the bodice.

Beautiful Back

Halters are the perfect "show off" top for you, especially if you wear your hair in an up do.

Willowy Legs

Short skirts should rule your world—wear them everywhere. Leggings and slim pants will play up their definition.

LOOKING THINNER IN A PHOTO

Place your hands on your hips so there's a space between your arms and your body.

Drop your chin and stick your tongue to the back roof of your mouth. It's what models do to define their jaw line.

Don't smile too broadly. It will cause your eyes to narrow, and will give you chipmunk cheeks. Smile as if you had fish hooks on either side of your mouth.

A BETTER BUTT

• Take the stairs. Contracting the muscles of the buttocks will firm and tone them quickly.

• Squeeze…squeeze…squeeze. Whether you're sitting at your desk or standing in line at the grocery store, squeeze your buttocks as hard as you possibly can. Count to ten, then release. Repeat as often as time allows.

• Lay off refined foods. Concentrate on whole grains and lean protein.

• Drinking a lot of water prevents a cushy tushy.

HINT: If you have a little too much "junk in your trunk," the one style you should absolutely stay away from is the dropped-style waist.

SLENDERIZE YOUR FEET

The right shoes can make your feet look an entire size smaller:

Wedges & platforms

Slender heels

Strappy sandals

Open toe styles

T-strap sandals (creates a vertical line from toe to ankle)

USE DETAILS TO CREATE A SLENDER LOOK

Although lots of clothing may look alike, there are subtle variations that can make a big difference in how it looks on you. So if you like a certain style, try on as many different manufacturers as you can find.

DISGUISE JIGGLY ARMS

• A V neckline draws attention away from less than perfect arms.

• Wear elbow-length sleeves, never capped.

• Throw a lightweight cardigan over a sleeveless dress.

MORE SLIM TIPS

Look great in a bikini by using self-tanner.

Wear heels. Even a one-inch heel will make legs look leaner.

Standing up straight makes you look thinner.

◀▶ HINT: The most slimming suit you can own is a long jacket with a below-the-knee skirt.

Petites

Don't wear anything too full or too long.

Wear short jackets.

Cinch in your clothing, particularly jackets and cardigans.

Slim trousers will lengthen your legs.

ANTI-BLOATING TECHNIQUES

Chew your food thoroughly. The slowler you eat, the less likely you are to suffer from gas.

Don't eat beans, cabbage, or cauliflower. They are the primary gas-producing foods.

Stay away from salt and salty foods. They cause puffiness from water retention.

Don't drink from a straw or chew gum. These bring air to the tummy. This is one of modeling's big rules. A model with a pot belly is not desirable.

Walk after eating to prevent bloating.

Stay away from carbonated beverages.

Don't eat anything with Sorbitol, a synthetic sugar. It's hard to digest and will cause bloating.

SLIMMING UNDERWEAR

Mini Control Slip

It's short enough to wear under a short skirt, and it helps eliminate bulges from waist to thigh.

Body-Shaper

This versatile slimmer comes with convertible, removable straps to work with any dress style to create a long, smooth line.

Body Shaping Slip

Look for the style with a structured underwire bra built in. It shapes the entire torso to eliminate any bulges or bumps.

STAR TRICKS FOR LOOKING THINNER

When actress **Teri Hatcher** gains weight, she immediately runs to the black and navy part of her wardrobe.

Talk show host **Joan Lunden** exercises in plastic sweats to lose temporary water weight.

Kathy Ireland and **Fran Drescher** are members of the bigger-the-hair-the-smaller-the-hips club.

DRESSING THINNER RULES
Keep patterns small.
Don't over-accessorize.
Go for simplicity.
Don't dress in layers.
Stay away from bulky shoulder pads and down coats.

Chapter 20

MODELS & CELEBRITIES

MODEL SECRETS

CLAUDIA SCHIFFER

When this 5-foot 11-inch model came to the United States she weighed around 140 pounds. Although this is an acceptable standard for German models, she needed to lose fifteen pounds in order to compete with the waif look happening here. Here's what she ate to get the fifteen pounds off.

Breakfast: Fruit juice and Grape Nuts with yogurt

Lunch: Soup, bread, and juice

Dinner: Chinese or French cuisine

Claudia admits that she struggles daily with a cookie addiction.

DAISY FUENTES

Former model and TV host Daisy Fuentes uses a quick weight loss trick she learned as a model. Drink one liter of chamomile tea and one liter of water daily. The combination accelerates fat-burning.

CINDY CRAWFORD

Cindy joins top Parisian models by using milk as a moisturizer. Her quick trick is to make a spritzer out of equal amounts of milk and water. She is known to refresh her face with it throughout the day.

PAMELA ANDERSON

How did this former *Baywatch* babe get her fabulous figure back after her two pregnancies? She swears her big secret is shea butter. She uses it all over her body, especially on the tummy area.

LEEZA GIBBONS

Talk show host Leeza Gibbons has fabulous hair, and when it needs a deep conditioning treatment she mixes together ¼ cup yogurt with an egg. She applies it to wet hair, wraps her head in a towel, and lets it set for a half hour before rinsing and shampooing.

MEG RYAN

When there's a movie coming up, Meg Ryan takes to the streets. She jogs or power walks three days a week and does yoga.

JENNIFER LOPEZ

When Jennifer Lopez appeared as a "fly girl" she was much heavier. Her curvaceous body is the result of leaving behind her mom's fried dishes and developing a strict fitness philosophy. She eats a breakfast of whole grain pancakes or toast with coffee, a shake for lunch, and a big salad with chicken, fish, or meat for dinner.

TYRA BANKS

Tyra battles a problem with flab with three-mile jogs.

COURTENEY COX

Courteney hates gyms but gets her body toned with ninety-minute yoga sessions.

NAOMI CAMPBELL

Count Naomi as one of the beautiful people relying on monthly power peels. It's a mild sanding of the skin's surface, creating an immediate rosy glow. The power peel softens lines and improves skin tone.

JENNA ELFMAN

This actress is a big believer in moisturizer. She applies a layer of moisturizer and allows it to dry before applying foundation. In this way, foundation goes on smoothly.

JENNIFER ANISTON

It's nice to hear that the celebrities struggle like we do. Jennifer Aniston admits that she has a slow metabolism and must stick to a diet of protein, vegetables, and monounsaturated fats. This is a far cry from her days of burgers, fries, and mayonnaise sandwiches.

JULIA ROBERTS

Although Julia Roberts has had personal trainers, she also works out privately with exercise videos. Since she bores easily, she likes to change them often.

LYNDA CARTER

Former Wonder Woman Lynda Carter zaps off ten pounds quickly by eating a healthy breakfast and dinner, and a yogurt for lunch.

BROOKE SHIELDS

When Brooke Shields needs to lose weight in a hurry, she turns to an interesting combination of V-8 juice and yeast.

SUSAN LUCCI

Soap opera actress Susan Lucci's favorite snack? It's sardines. She eats them for their omega-3 fatty acids, essential for smooth skin.

JENNIFER LOVE HEWITT

Hewitt applies toothpaste to her pimples overnight.

MICHELLE YEOH

This actress rinses her face in lemon juice and water.

KIRSTIE ALLEY

Don't you love Kirstie Alley's highlights? She does them herself! She applies facial hair bleach with a tooth brush. It's fast, working in less than ten minutes.

ELIZABETH HURLEY

Elizabeth Hurley's secret for keeping thin is to eat with a miniature set of knives and forks. She even brings them to restaurants.

DEFYING AGE

Sophia Loren is the doyen of discipline. For years, she has talked about her love of pasta, but before you start digging in, listen to what she doesn't eat. Sophia rarely eats meat, and drinks lots of water. You won't find her eating potato chips, smoking cigarettes, or drinking an alcoholic beverage. Cheese, fruit, and vegetables make up the rest of her daily meals.

How does "Supreme" diva **Diana Ross** stay in shape? She does her own housework. "Cleaning is a tremendous stress reliever and it keeps my body taut," says Diana. Any twenty-five-year-old would have a hard time competing with this 5-foot 4-inch, one hundred-pound fifty-three-year-old.

Yoga plays a major role in the wonderful condition **Raquel Welch** is in at age fifty-seven. She practices some form of it every day. She is a big protein eater (turkey, veal, fish, some red meat), and her snacks include rice cakes and fresh fruit.

Stirring honey into her coffee or tea helps **Ann-Margret** stay away from sweets. This motorcycle-driving actress and singer watches her diet by avoiding soda, candy, and peanuts. She also reportedly went on a watermelon diet for two weeks to drop twenty pounds. She ate watermelon for breakfast and lunch along with lots of water. At dinner, she would eat a low-fat, nourishing meal.

No snacks for former "Mamas and Papas" singer and _Knots Landing_ actress **Michelle Phillips**. This fifty-four-year-old owes her 5-foot 7-inch, one hundred-twenty-pound figure to fresh fruit and vegetables, supplemented by daily vitamins.

Faye Dunaway claims she is in better condition today at age fifty-six than at any other time in her life. There is no white flour in her diet, just lots of salads, grilled fish, vegetables, and seven-grain breads.

Melanie Griffith eats nothing but fruit in the mornings when she's trying to lose weight.

When actress **Joan Collins** needs to lose weight quickly to flatten her tummy into a slinky *Dynasty* type gown, she'll stop eating for an entire day. Other times, all it takes is to eliminate one dinner.

Chapter 21

FAST-LANE BEAUTY

WHEN THERE'S NO TIME

Beauty on the run? Yes, you can do it. There's no excuse to turn down that last-minute invitation. There's no reason for looking like you've just come out of a wind tunnel. Life has become hectic, and beauty in a hurry has become the norm. After all, who has the time for all-day preparation. It's time to start simplifying your entire beauty routine. What once took an afternoon can now be done in just minutes.

DON'T WASTE TIME

Don't worry about looking perfect. Just jump in and do it.

FIX HAIR FAST

Add instant volume to short hair by working mousse through hair, then drying with a diffuser.

Make long hair look thicker by bending over at the waist and brushing hair. This injects air into the roots and makes them stand up. Use hair spray at roots first for even more lift.

Create Instantly Sleek Hair

1. Dry hair about 80 percent at roots.

2. Set on Velcro rollers.

3. Leave in fifteen minutes.

HINT: Cut blow-drying time by dividing hair into sections. Lift at the roots with paddle brush or round brush. In warm weather you can get away with leaving hair slightly damp.

NO TIME TO SHAMPOO

• Mist hair with water to bring back some of its natural texture. Comb through with fingers.

• Mist a little water on hair and spot blow-dry.

• Spray on a leave-in conditioner and style.

• Rub scalp with facial toner.

Quick Shine

Invigorate scalp by using a natural bristle brush. Distribute oils by brushing from scalp to ends.

Frizz Tamer

Rub canola oil between palms and rub over hair. This is an oil rich in vitamin E. Lack of vitamin E is one of the primary causes of frizziness.

No Time to Dry

You can skip the blow-drying altogether if you style your hair with a wide-tooth comb while it's still wet. Towel dry and make a side part. Comb a glossing gel through hair, smoothing as you go. Then just pull back behind your ears, and make a low ponytail.

HINT: Use a metal core brush when blow-drying. It cuts time in half because the metal retains heat.

QUICK COSMETICS

No Toothbrush

Just rinse your mouth with water. The Academy of General Dentistry reports that it helps neutralize acids and reduces bacteria.

Do Two Things At Once

Save time by tweezing eyebrows while waiting for hair color to develop, or let your pedicure dry while applying eyeliner.

Rush the Blush

Smile and brush over area that's most prominent, then blend in. This is the quickest way to hit exactly the right spot.

Fast Nails

Dress up nails by adding a layer of sheer pearl polish to whatever color you're already wearing.

Bare nails are better than chipped. If your nails can't be touched up, remove your color and smooth any rough edges with an emery board.

HINT: Give your freshly polished nails a quick spritz of nonstick cooking spray to cut down on their drying time.

Two-for-One Makeup

Foundation works as a concealer when dipping into the cap with a brush.

Sheer lipsticks highlight and blush.

Powder eye shadow can be applied with a damp brush as an eyeliner. That's any eyeshadow, it's not necessary to be labled wet/dry.

Use clear mascara to control eyebrows.

Tinted moisturizer acts as a moisturizer, sunscreen, and foundation.

GET DRESSED QUICKLY

Put clothes away in ready-to-go condition so there are no surprises to slow you down. If there's no time to iron, wear knits.

GET OUT THE DOOR FAST

1. Ditch the morning cleansing routine. As I've said many times, a cool splash of water is all you need. It boosts circulation and creates a morning glow.

2. Use your fingers to apply eye shadow. You will achieve a sheer, natural look in seconds with no hard lines.

3. Line only the outer corner of the eye when you're pressed for time.

4. Apply lipstick with your finger. It will create a sheer glossy look. Any residue becomes a quick, subtle blush.

HINT: If you find that you've gone too heavy on your shadow, lipstick or blush, run a bit of white shadow over the area to lighten up.

ONE COLOR/LESS HASSLE

Use monochromatic makeup to look finished when there's just no time. Apply bronze lipstick as a shadow, blush, and lip color. You can even use it as a highlighter on your nose and forehead, or any other area the sun would naturally color.

PLAN AHEAD

Use beauty products conveniently packaged like flip tops, capsules, and pads.

Face-blotting papers are quicker to use than compacts.

Keep one casual and one business outfit ready to go.

Keep skin-care items in a basket on your bathroom counter so it's convenient and your routine becomes almost unconscious.

Never have more than two eye shadows and three lipsticks laying out.

Have cotton swabs ready to tidy up smudges.

NO TIME TO EXERCISE?

1. Carry a jump rope with you and try to get in a few minutes when you can.
2. Wear ankle weights when you're watching TV or talking on the phone.
3. Keep five-pound weights at your desk to work your arms.

Chapter 22

BEAUTY ON A BUDGET

WHEN MONEY IS TIGHT

There's no reason you can't combine beauty with a tight budget. It may take a bit more time, but it's amazing how much you can save. Many of the name-brand cosmetic counter products you've been relying on for years have inexpensive counterparts. Once you learn to read labels and explore alternative avenues, you'll never want to go back to overspending.

TAKE CHARGE OF YOUR MONEY

• Don't shop at stores that don't offer a full refund policy.

• Check out mass merchandisers for basics.

• If you find something on sale that you paid full price for, bring it back with the receipt for a price adjustment.

• Leave tags on for two to three days to make sure you really want it.

• Keep a list in your purse of needed items so you stay on track.

SHOP FOR FREE AT COSMETIC COUNTERS

The next time you're looking for some free samples, just head to your favorite cosmetic counters. They usually have a treasure trove of products that are free if you ask. Your best bet is to look through the fashion magazines and check out the latest products. When a product comes out, the cosmetic company will stock their counter people with samples to hand out. This is part of their marketing approach, to get women to try out a product, get results, and come back and purchase the full size.

If you're just dying to try a product, and there's no samples available, buy it anyway. If it doesn't work, you should be able to go back and get a full refund. Don't waste your money with a worthless product.

Go sample shopping during slow times. The counter person may be more generous. Call ahead to see what samples might be available.

DO YOU REALLY NEED IT?

Start buffing your nails for a more natural look. Or use clear nail polish instead of colors. It looks better longer, without touch ups.

Start wearing a hairstyle that works with your natural hair. You'll save a lot of money on hair-styling products.

SHOP SECOND-HAND

Period clothes often come in wonderful fabric and are usually far better made than their modern equivalents. You will also get more for your money. For the cost of one new designer dress, you can purchase the dress, all the accessories, and probably a coat.

Check underarm areas and seams carefully. If an item looks terribly stained or torn, or needs anything more than cleaning, a little tailoring, or new buttons, then pass it by.

Always be sure to keep shapes simple. They are the styles that can be most easily altered.

Look for jackets, tops, and coats. They have the most "forgivable" fit, and are easiest to try on. Most resale shops don't have dressing rooms.

Check out consignment shops in affluent neighborhoods. They're more likely to have designer clothing.

Resale shops in cities with apparel marts may also carry designer samples; lucky you if you wear a size six or eight.

HINT: See if the hem line of the garment has enough material to repair a tear.

MAKE YOUR PRODUCTS LAST LONGER

Add water to shampoos and conditioners to get the very last from the bottles.

You can add a drop of water to a water-soluble mascara wand when it gets dry to loosen and mix mascara.

Add nail polish thinner to old nail polish. Polish tends to gather in the bottom of the bottle.

Mix foundation with a little moisturizer to get a more natural look.

IS IT REALLY A BARGAIN?

Be aware that if you buy something on sale, you may need to purchase other pieces to make the item work. You need to work that figure into the cost.

When items go on sale or are last season's style at a discount store, you may need to have them dry cleaned to freshen them up. That also needs to be added to the cost.

GO BACK TO SCHOOL

If you daydream of a manicure or a soothing massage, but you just don't have the money, call a student clinic. Virtually all schools that teach hairstylists, nail technicians, massage therapists, etc., look for "real" people on which they can teach their techniques. Although prices vary, they are nominal. A $100 hair coloring may cost $20 at the school, and a massage may be only $5, or even free.

Call before you go. Most schools have limited hours.

Don't be afraid that a first-timer will be working on you. Students almost always are supervised by highly skilled teachers.

FREE DENTAL ADVICE

Got a dental question? Submit your question to the Academy of General Dentistry's Web site at www.agd.org, and a dentist will respond within twenty-four hours.

BROKEN COMPACT

If you've dropped your pressed powder compact, and it's fallen apart, don't throw it away.

Break up the remaining chunks and add a small amount of rubbing alcohol. Mix it until it forms a paste. Press it back into the compact. In a few hours the alcohol will evaporate, leaving a solid cake.

Drugstores vs. Cosmetic Counters

Most cosmetic counter companies will argue that their products contain more dense pigments for a more intense color and a longer lasting finish. Those results come from application and the type of brush used. Go to an art supply store to get high quality brushes. The variety is endless.

I have tracked down factories that admit to selling to both drugstores and to high-end companies. Very often the only difference is in the packaging.

SHOPPING MECCAS

Girls' and teen departments: hair accessories and fun jewelry

Men's department: tee shirts

Ethnic supermarkets: unusual shoes and bags, herbs

INTERNET SITES:

www.justfreestuff.com

www.freestuffcentral.com

www.freestuff.com

HAIR SAVINGS

Models swear by OXY 10 to add highlights to their hair.

Use no more than ¼ cup shampoo and you don't need a second sudsing.

BARGAIN ALL-DAY LIPSTICK

Mash raw beets and apply with a cotton swab.

Cherry lip balm gives a natural-looking stain.

Chapter 23

BEAUTY ON THE ROAD

BRING BEAUTY WITH YOU

There's no reason to let your looks go when you do. Simplify when you travel—yes, leave it all behind—no.

PICK TWO

That's two colors, max. This takes a lot of restraint, but it makes packing a matter of minutes, rather than hours.

WATCH THE SHOES

Keep your packing light by paring down your shoes. Shoes take up lots of room. You need one pair of dress heels plus a walking shoe. That's it unless you're going to a resort. Add a pair of sandals for beachwear.

CORE PACKING LIST

Umbrella

Bathing suit

Sweater

Raincoat

Leggings

Dress

Sunglasses

Sneakers

Jacket

Never Pack

Linen

Jeans (weigh too much)

Hair dryers (all hotels have them)

Iron

HOW TO PACK

Put shoes in ripped hose or plastic bags.

Roll everything.

Stick with a list.

Never bring a full-size container of any product, including medicine.

Make your suitcase bottom-heavy.

Button and zipper everything to fight wrinkling.

Stuff shoes with belts, hosiery, underwear, and jewelry.

Bring plastic supermarket bags to hold wet and dirty items.

Pack tight. Loose clothing wrinkles.

Bring along a foldable bag for souvenirs.

SAVE FILM CONTAINERS

Use film containers to pack just the right amount of shampoo, conditioner, jewelry, medication, and other small items.

ONE PRODUCT, MANY USES

Use shampoo as a body wash and detergent for fine washables.
Baby wipes remove makeup and stains, and refresh skin.
Body lotion doubles as a leave-in hair conditioner.

HINT: Some items like shampoos, lotions, etc., can open under airplane pressure. Pack them in plastic bags.

LEG WORK

Phone your hotel and ask about gym facilities on site or nearby. Inquire about nearby parks, running tracks, hiking trails, tennis courts, and other exercising options. Ask if there are shuttle services to some of these areas. Even shuttles to shopping areas are good for a spirited "mall-walk."

MAKE RESERVATIONS

Call your airline and ask about special meals. Every airline will offer an alternative, and your best bet is vegetarian or low-fat. Some even offer cold seafood, all fruit, and Hindu (a baked potato and steamed vegetables).

Chapter 24

ILLNESS EMERGENCIES

LOOK YOUR BEST

Whether an illness is of the twenty-four-hour flu variety or possibly life-threatening, recovery can be enhanced by feeling good about our surroundings and our looks. Makeup not only has the ability to camouflage problems, but can boost our morale. If you've never worn makeup before, try out a few products and techniques now. If you have a makeup regime, it may be necessary to make a few changes.

WATCH HOW YOU WASH

Radiation

During radiation therapy, it's vitally important not to wash off any marks that your doctor or radio therapist may have applied to your skin. These marks will eventually fade away. Use only warm water (not too hot or too cold) in the treatment areas. Never rub your skin. Ever-so-gently pat it dry instead.

Chemotherapy

Some chemotherapy patients have experienced extremely dry skin. Unless you're removing makeup or dirt, stay away from heavy cleansers or soaps. Lukewarm water splashed several times, and blotted dry with a fluffy towel, will suffice.

SKIN AND NAIL CARE

With any illness, skin is the first to suffer. Put some color back in your cheeks even before your blush goes on.

Skin Care Routine

1. Cleanse by using warm (never hot) water with a creamy cleanser. Try to stay away from soaps (too irritating to traumatized skin).

2. Moisturize with a rich moisturizer infused with a vitamin A capsule. Not only are you nourishing

your skin, but it will create a smooth surface for your makeup.

3. A moisturizing foundation will give your face a natural-looking glow. You may need heavier coverage to even out your complexion.

4. Set your foundation with a light coating of powder, applied with a large, fluffy brush.

5. You absolutely need blush or bronzing powder at this time. Contouring with a bronzing powder or brown-toned blush will disguise puffiness due to weight gain or treatment. A light pink or peach blush will induce a healthy glow. Stay away from harsh colors like reds, deep pinks, or purples.

Nail Care

Certain drugs, or processes like chemotherapy, can cause changes in nails and the nail bed. You may find your nails more brittle, discolored, and grooved. There may be a change in your nail's growth and the nail bed itself may lift.

• Keep your nails somewhat short for both appearance and safety.

• Massage cuticle cream or vitamin E into the cuticle area to prevent dryness, splitting, and hang nails.

• Don't cut your cuticles. Push them back instead.

• Try to wear gloves when doing housework, especially when your hands will be in water (such as washing dishes). Excessive exposure to water can lead to fungal infections of the nail bed.

• Use nail polish or clear nail shield to keep nails strong and protected from the environment.

• Use an oily, formaldehyde-free nail polish remover. Nails may have become weak or brittle during illness or treatment.

• Avoid nails that have to be glued on.

THE FACE

Eyebrows

In a very serious illness, eyebrows may thin or fall out entirely. Find your natural brow arch and use short feathery strokes for a natural look.

HINT: Find a close-up photograph of yourself before your illness or treatment began.

1. Use a brush-on eyebrow color or pencil in your present hair or wig color.

2. Hold the pencil straight up against your nose, parallel to the inside corner of your eye. This is where the eyebrow should begin.

3. Draw a dot just above the brow bone.

4. Look straight ahead and place the pencil parallel to the outside edge of the colored part of the eye. Place a dot where the highest point of the browline should be.

5. Place the pencil diagonally from the bottom corner of your nose past the outside corner of your eye, and draw a dot. This will show you where the outside edge should go.

HINT: Be sure the outer edge of the brow is not lower than the inside one so that a sullen look is not created.

6. Connect the dots into a brow line with a soft pencil.

Eyes

The right eye makeup can brighten your eyes considerably.

1. Apply highlighter just below the brow arch.

2. Sweep a complementary eye shadow (don't go too dark) color across the entire lid.

3. Add a darker color in the crease of the eyes and on the top lash line and under the lower lash line.

4. Apply a soft eyeliner to define the eye and give the illusion of eyelashes where there are none or where they have become sparse.

5. Consider wearing false eyelashes. With practice, they can can look just like your own. They may need to be thinned and trimmed to look natural.

6. Curling lashes combined with the use of mascara can make eyes look bigger and more alert.

Lips

Attention brought to the lips will take it away from the more obvious areas of fatigue. Lipstick can also disguise any medicinal stains.

• Outline lips with a soft pencil to prevent "bleeding" and define edges.

• Match or complement lip and blush color.

• Choose a lipstick with long-lasting or "all-day" labeling. If your lips are very dry, apply petroleum jelly or lip balm first.

HAIR

Hair Loss

The most obvious and distressing change that illness or treatment may cause is the loss of hair. The good news is that with today's more advanced treatments most people don't lose all their hair.

Get a Good Haircut

A shorter cut can make your hair look thicker. Save a lock of your hair so that you can match the color later if you should decide to get a wig.

HINT: If you are receiving radiation treatment, you may actually find longer hair easier to style. It will allow for coverage of thinning areas.

Avoid Chemicals

Until your hair has grown out completely, perms, coloring, and straightening should wait. Use gentle shampoos, nourishing conditioners, and styling products.

Wigs

Today's variety of wigs is endless. There are both synthetic and human hair in all price ranges. Plan to take some time to try on several styles before making your selection. Bring a friend or your hairstylist to help you decide. To ensure comfort and fit, try to go to a professional with a long-standing, positive reputation.

Custom-made wigs are common, and usually can be created for around $300. Your insurance may cover the cost, especially if your doctor recommends it. The American Cancer Society also provides wigs in some circumstances. For more information, call them at (800) 227-2345.

SUPPORT AND SPECIALTY SHOPS

General Cancer Support

Your hospital will provide valuable local support information. Also call (800) 4-CANCER for information and literature.

Many hospitals will have a "Look Good...Feel Better" program in place. It's a free, national public service program created from the concept that if a woman with cancer can be helped to look good, her improved self-esteem will help her approach her disease and treatment with greater confidence. The program offers free makeup kits and information on how to use them to get you through your worst days. It is open to all women cancer patients actively undergoing cancer treatment. More than two hundred thousand women have participated since its inception. Call (800) 395-LOOK for more information.

Breast Cancer Support

Y-ME will connect you with a breast cancer survivor and give you information on support groups in your area as well as information on starting your own support group if you prefer. Their national support hotline phone number is (800) 221-2141.

Post-Mastectomy Fitting

Look in your local phone book if your hospital's social worker doesn't have a reference for post-mastectomy bra fitting. Here's one I found that impressed me because of the owner's willingness to answer any questions regardless of whether I purchased anything from her. (Please note that if you do visit New York, her location is not a storefront.) Also, make sure you establish privacy issues when you call your local shop for information.

Reflections Mastectomy Boutique

36 East 36th Street
New York, NY 10016
(212) 679-2160
www.reflections-boutique.com

Total Woman Boutique

The following Web site is impressive in its information on insurance possibilities as well as suggested reading.

Visit them at www.thetotalwomanboutique.com or call (877) 849-6626 for a free catalog.

Carry Lifesaving Information

No longer do you have to wear those institutional wristbands. Slim Line Products, Inc. has developed an SOS locket. Available as necklaces, bracelets, and key chains, it carries a lot of information with style. Prices range from $39.50 to $79.50. Call them at (800) 224-3535 or look them up on the Internet at www.slimline.com.

Hair Loss Help

Locks of Love is a charity that provides hair pieces to financially disadvantaged children and teens under the age of eighteen that are experiencing medical hair loss.

Call them at (561) 963-1677.

Write them at: *Locks of Love*
Suite 104
Palm Springs, FL 33461

SURROUND YOURSELF WITH BEAUTY AND LOVE

Don't forget to pamper yourself a little to help keep the environment around you comfortable. Continued beauty and pride in your surroundings will go a long way toward boosting your mental outlook.

Spray your bed linens with rose water.

Add a few drops of eucalyptus (available at health food stores and natural supermarkets) to promote breathing and aid sleep.

Try to stay with natural fragrances to prevent nausea.

Treat yourself to flowers, but don't keep them too long.

Use potpourri generously, especially lavender, in the bathroom and bedroom.

Chapter 25

COSMETIC QUICK FIXES

BEAUTY GONE WRONG

How do you solve that unforeseen beauty crisis? You do it right away. You use the most inventive techniques available, with whatever product you can find that works.

SKIN SOLUTIONS

Acne

There's nothing like a pimple to ruin a look. And models learn at a very early age how to deal with them on the spot.

Calamine Lotion

If your pimples are rash-like, apply calamine lotion and let dry overnight.

Eye Redness Reliever

Just as it gets the redness out of the eyes, it quickly eliminates the redness from the pimple. The pimple is still there, but it is invisible.

Tea Tree Oil

It's the best antiseptic for dealing with pimples. Drop a little on a cotton swab and hold it to the pimple for a minute or two.

Toothpaste

Take a little toothpaste (not gel, it doesn't work) and dab it on your pimple. Leave it on overnight.

Saliva

Spit on your finger and apply to zit. Saliva is a powerful antiseptic.

Salt

Combine ¼ teaspoon table salt with one cup lukewarm water. Dip a piece of gauze into the mixture, then lightly press it against the blemish for one minute. The salt solution will help bring down swelling and eliminate redness.

Enlarged Pores

Tighten them with a paste made from a packet of yeast moistened with just enough lemon juice to make a paste.

Back Break Outs

Wash area with dishwashing detergent. Yes, what it does for dishes (cuts the grease) it can do for back and chest breakouts. Apply it with a bath brush, not with your hands.

Follow with an application of benzoyl peroxide.

Major Breakout Emergency

Rub half a potato all over your face. Leave the raw potato juice on for twenty to thirty minutes. Rinse with cold water.

Dull Skin

Spritz face with equal parts cold water and witch hazel. Finish with tinted moisturizer. Don't use face masks more than once a week. They cause flaking.

Red, Blotchy Legs

The shin bone is difficult to shave because the bone is pointed, and the razor is flat. Shave the flat sides of the bone, rather than the center of the shin.

Apply a leave-in hair conditioner to get a smoother shave. Some shaving gels can cause irritation and redness.

Rash Reliever

Take two aspirin (an anti-inflammatory), then apply a cold milk compress to the affected area.

Bikini Line Rash

Apply a whole milk compress for five minutes.

If a rash is bad enough, ask a dermatologist for a prescription of Erythromycin. Apply and let set for twenty minutes. Rinse.

Waxing Irritation

Apply yogurt to irritated area for about ten to fifteen minutes.

Blot a wet tea bag on affected area.

Fading Tan

Mix loose gold powder or bronzing powder with body lotion. Smooth over skin.

Tan Streaks

Rub toothpaste into those odd orange stripes.

Stressed Out Skin

Spread vitamin E oil over entire face. Cover face with plastic wrap, making holes for nose and mouth. Leave for fifteen to twenty minutes. Rinse off with warm water.

Sallow Skin

Add purple eye shadow to foundation or moisturizer. The purple color conceals yellow undertones.

HEALTH AND WELLNESS

Puffy Eyes

Run a spoon under cold water and apply metal to puffiness.

Apply a bag of frozen vegetables to the area.

Freeze a baby's teething ring and rest on puffiness for five minutes.

Wake up your entire face by putting it in front of an open freezer and counting to one hundred. That's what makeup artists do to sleepy models.

Warts

Puncture a vitamin A capsule, mix with a drop of lemon juice, and apply directly to the wart.

Cold Sores

There are medications for cold sores and fever blisters. If you don't have any on hand, apply a slightly dampened aspirin to the sore. Hold it there for at least three minutes.

Keep the sore and its surrounding area clean and dry to fight bacteria.

Eat a bland diet, avoiding chocolate, nuts, or gelatin-based products. These foods may irritate the sore and cause further infection.

Breath Fresheners

Drink water with lemon.

Brush your tongue.

Eat an apple to clean away leftover particles.

Dingy Teeth

Mix baking soda and hydrogen peroxide as an emergency cleaner. Stay away from sensitive gum area.

Sweaty Palms

Rub a powder-based deodorant over palms.

Spray palms with perfume.

HANGOVER HELPERS

Morning-After Face

If your beauty emergency is a night that lasted a little too long, you'll need to pull out a few tricks. Well, maybe more than just a few.

1. If you forgot to take off your makeup before you went to bed, use a gentle remover, not soap.

2. If you have any pimples, don't squeeze them. Your skin is probably still puffy and sensitive.

3. Use an oil-free moisturizer or a tinted moisturizer. Blend with your fingers to start blood flow, while gently "piano tapping" under the eyes.

4. Drink lots of water to wash away bloating and toxins and to replace that lost fluid.

5. Pull hair up in a tight ponytail so it pulls bags away from the eye area.

Get Some Air

If it's possible, try to get out into the sunlight and get some exercise. It will work the alcohol out of your system (actually it will metabolize it) by increasing your intake of oxygen.

Carry a Spritzer

Refresh your face throughout the day by carrying a spritzer bottle filled with chamomile tea that has cooled. The chamomile will calm down the redness of your face, while the water will keep you hydrated.

HINT: If you don't have a spritzer on hand, dampen a washcloth with cold water, and gently dab at your face. It will soothe the skin, while hydrating. Do this throughout the day.

Wear Sunglasses

No sarcasm intended here. You may find that your eyes are not only puffy, but sensitive to the sun.

How to Apply Makeup

1. Use a light-reflecting concealer under the eyes and toward inner corners.

2. Sweep a neutral color or nude eye shadow over lids. You wouldn't want anyone to concentrate on those red eyes.

3. Bring attention up and away from the redness by highlighting the brow bone with a light-colored shadow or white pencil.

4. Use a brown liner on upper lash line and into the crease of the eye. Then smudge it with a cotton swab. Curl lashes and lightly coat with mascara.

5. Apply a bronzing powder or bronzing cream. Stay away from pinks, which make tired skin look even more irritated.

6. Avoid powder if possible, but if your face requires it, choose a yellow-based translucent powder applied with a large, fluffy brush.

Your Lips Will Never Tell

If there's one spot that should be defined, it's the mouth. It's the only area of the face that doesn't carry tales. Be bold with color, and make the eye bypass your flaws and go to your lips. Choose a blue-based red or soft coral or brown. Stay away from mattes, which are too drying. Instead, choose a moisturizing formula, which will carry a slight shine.

HINT: If you line your lips after applying lipstick, it will allow for a softer definition.

Your lips may be parched or chapped, so gently brush them with a soft toothbrush before your lipstick goes on.

MAKEUP MIRACLES

Emergency Face Lifts

Take an egg white and gently pat all over face. Don't move a muscle until it dries. Gently tissue off excess. It will keep your face firm until you wash it off.

Hemorrhoid cream shrinks and takes down the swelling from those other cheeks, and that's what it does for puffy eyes and a droopy jawline. Be careful of the eye area, and for the hemorrhoid cream to work, it must include both yeast and shark's liver oil.

Applying Lipstick Without a Mirror

Carefully dab lipstick along bottom lip and on the bow of your upper lip. Rub lips together to blend.

Bleeding Lipstick

Use concealer all around your mouth to prevent lipstick from bleeding.

Broken Lipstick

When lipstick snaps off its case it can be easily repaired. Hold the broken end over a lit match. Push the lipstick back on the case. Store it in the refrigerator overnight to set.

Mascara Smudge

Dip a cotton swab into makeup remover and gently dab smear away. Blend back foundation with a damp sponge.

Out of Concealer

1. Use cream-colored eye shadow.

2. Dip into the cap of your foundation. It's a thicker consistency, just like concealer, and just the right color.

Whoops! You've lost your brow pencil

Use a #2 pencil. Sharpen it to a fine point, and use short, feathery strokes. Be careful not to break the skin.

A powder eye shadow pencil provides soft definition.

HAIR HAZARDS

Greasy Hair

Add a teaspoon of aloe vera gel to shampoo application.

Dandruff

Mix together:

capful of apple cider vinegar

capful of vodka

2 drops tea tree oil

¾ cup warm water

Rub into scalp after shampooing and conditioning. Don't rinse out.

Split Ends

Massage maple syrup into dry hair.

Cover with a shower cap for thirty minutes.

Shampoo twice.

Emergency Hair Gel

Boil two teaspoons of sugar with ½ cup water. Let cool, and apply to hair.

Ouch! Hair Is Tangled in Curling Iron, Brush, Roller...

Try to unravel one or two strands at a time. Use a rat tail comb to pull ends off.

FEEL-GOOD FEET

Emergency Shoe Shine

Pour a little hand lotion on a paper towel or tissue, and wipe over shoes.

Tired Feet

Soak feet in a mixture of three tablespoons mustard and one quart warm water. Mustard is reduces swelling and soreness.

EMERGENCY NAILS

Your Manicure Has Become Dull

Rub a little olive oil on each nail, and your nails will appear freshly polished.

Nail Polish Gone Bad

Add two or three drops of polish remover to the bottle and gently shake.

Out of Polish Remover—Use Insect Repellent

This tip came about accidentally during a swimsuit photo shoot in the Caribbean. The bugs started biting, so out came the repellent. We all had fabulously painted nails on our hands and feet which came right off. Who knew?

No insect repellent around? Like removes like. Polish over painted nails and quickly wipe off.

TIPS FROM PAGEANT CONTESTANTS

I've worked with many different pageants, and I assure you, that from Miss Hawaiian Tropic to Mrs. USA, when it comes to winning, they pull out every stop.

Lift breasts with duct tape to play up cleavage.

Apply hemorrhoid cream to upper legs to shrink them, then wrap them in plastic wrap.

Apply strong coffee grounds to cellulite, and then further smoothing it out with a rolling pin.

Apply petroleum jelly to teeth for a broad smile.

Chapter 26

EMERGENCY DIETS

WHEN YOU NEED TO GET IT OFF FAST!

A crash diet isn't always a bad thing, and they really work if you can dedicate yourself for a day or two. Emergency diets have the ability to inspire the dieter by the quick results seen over just a few days. Although the weight loss is mostly water, some fat is also lost. The other benefits are a flatter stomach, a sense of well-being, and reduced bulges around the hips and thighs. I have included some of this information in my other books, and these diet programs are among the most requested of me over the years, so I've included them here for your benefit. As always, I recommend you consult your doctor before embarking on diets and other potentially dramatic changes to your body.

THE ONE-DAY JUICE FAST

This diet is probably the most popular "one day only" diet (besides fasting) that has been used to drop about two to three pounds in one day without using any supplements. Fresh juices have great nutritional value, and contain important enzymes, minerals, and vitamins. They cleanse your system, and make you feel like you could conquer the world!

7 A.M.: A cup of hot water with the juice of one lemon or one teaspoon of reconstituted lemon juice

8 A.M.: Apple-Carrot Juice consisting of four unpeeled carrots and two unpeeled, cored apples

10 A.M.: A glass of water or a cup of herbal tea

12 P.M.: A large glass of grapefruit juice and a large glass of ice water

2 P.M.: A glass of water and a cup of herbal tea

4 P.M.: A glass of pineapple juice and a glass of ice water

6 P.M.: Herbal tea and a glass of water

8 P.M.: Pineapple or grapefruit juice with a glass of ice water

10 P.M.: A cup of hot water with juice of one lemon or one teaspoon of reconstituted lemon

If you find that you have a difficult time getting to sleep after a day of this juice diet, try adding a few special herbs to your bath. Visit your local health food store, where you'll find oils to help you relax. Look for essences of rose, sandalwood, and lavender. To enjoy wonderfully natural aromatherapy, just cut up a lemon or orange and throw it in. These are the basis of citric cleaners, and will make your bathtub shine! Herbal tea bags also create a relaxing bath treatment. Especially soothing are cloves, peppermint, and chamomile.

THE GRAPEFRUIT DIET

This is a diet that doesn't require a lot of planning or thought. You don't need to count calories or make major food decisions. The plus side to this diet is that grapefruit contains so much fiber and water, it fills you up quickly. The downside is that it's too restrictive to be healthy for more than a couple of days.

Breakfast: Half a grapefruit with coffee or tea

Lunch: Two eggs, lettuce, and tomato salad spritzed with lemon and vinegar, a slice of toast, half a grapefruit, and coffee or tea

Dinner: Fish or chicken, half a grapefruit, cucumbers or tomatoes, and coffee or tea

THE MINI MEAL DIET

Eating food only three times a day, at breakfast, lunch, and dinner is too restricting for many dieters. Being able to "graze" throughout the day, especially when cutting drastically back on calories, ups the success rate radically. This plan allows for eating six times a day, and still will yield an average weight loss of five to six pounds in three days. It's easy to follow, and really quite painless!

Menu One

Breakfast: one cup Frosted Shredded Wheat with skim milk, coffee or tea

Snack: ½ cup cubed cantaloupe or one apple

Lunch: four ounces sliced turkey breast on whole grain bread with one teaspoon mustard

Mixed green salad

Coffee, tea, or diet soda

Snack: one cup skim milk

one chocolate chip cookie

Dinner: 3 oz. broiled chicken or fish

one cup cooked spinach

coffee, tea, or ice water

Snack: 6 oz. low-fat yogurt

Menu Two

Breakfast: ½ cup strawberries

6 oz. low-fat yogurt

coffee or tea

Snack: ½ cup baby carrots

6 pretzels

Lunch: one cup canned vegetable soup

4 saltine crackers

Coffee, tea, or diet soda

Snack: one apple

Dinner: 3 oz. sirloin steak

one cup sliced green beans

coffee, tea, or iced water

Snack: ½ cup low-fat frozen yogurt

This diet works quickly and efficiently because you know that you'll be eating again in just two hours. Those of us who are parents know that when our children are young, it's important to bring along snacks if we plan to be away from home for a long period of time. Yet, we never anticipate our own hunger, which can lead to that stop at the vending machine, fast food drive-in, and the downfall of our best intentions of the morning. Snacking is important for restoring energy as well as staving off hunger pains.

THE SPA THREE-DAY DIET

Try this diet on a relaxing weekend. It's sure to bring a satisfying five- to six-pound weight loss. Try to incorporate it into a "makeover" time for you. Wear your workout clothes and take a hike around your neighborhood. Test out those homemade masks and hair treatments you've been anxious, but too busy, to try.

Day One

Breakfast

two frozen low fat waffles topped with ½ cup blueberries and a teaspoon of low-fat topping

coffee or tea

Lunch

one cup mixed greens with one oz. water-packed tuna and 2 tbs. low-fat dressing or mayonnaise

alfalfa sprouts and red peppers to taste

one slice protein or whole grain bread

Diet beverage

Dinner

3 oz. chicken breast coated with one tbs. each Dijon mustard, honey, and apple-cider vinegar

sprinkle with basil and broil

2 cup mixed greens topped with 2 tbs. low-fat dressing

coffee or tea

Day Two

Breakfast

½ grapefruit

one slice pita bread toasted with one oz. Swiss or Muenster cheese

coffee or tea

Lunch

Mix ¼ cup grapes, pineapple slices, kiwi, and strawberries with one cup yogurt. Sprinkle with 2 tsp. wheat germ.

diet beverage, coffee, or tea

Dinner

one cup pasta of choice topped with ½ cup marinara sauce and one tsp. parmesan cheese

one cup steamed zucchini

2 cup mixed greens tossed with 2 Tbs. low-fat dressing

coffee or tea

Day Three

Breakfast

one slice raisin bread broiled with one tbs. low fat cottage cheese topped with cinnamon

¼ cup fruit

coffee or tea

Lunch

one slice pita bread broiled with one oz. mozzarella cheese, sliced tomatoes, and your choice of mushrooms, broccoli, and onions.

2 cup mixed greens with 2 tbs. low fat dressing

diet beverage

Dinner

3 oz. white fish broiled with one tsp. sesame oil and sesame seeds, topped with ginger

½ cup wild rice

one cup broccoli

coffee, tea, or diet beverage

Each day choose two of the following snacks:

one cup cubed cantaloupe

½ cup banana blended with ½ cup skim milk, one tsp. vanilla, and 4 ice cubes

½ cup skim milk and one low-fat cookie

THE ULTIMATE JUMP-START DIET

THE GARLIC AND PAPAYA DIET

This is a totally natural diuretic that can be used when you need to get into an outfit quickly and safely. Many models use it to prepare for a photo shoot. This is the "secret" formula behind very expensive capsules being sold in Hollywood.

Take two garlic tablets and two papaya tablets before breakfast, lunch, and dinner. Eat lightly for two days, staying away from salt, bread, and carbonated beverages. Stay near a bathroom because this will draw fluids (safely) from your body.

To accelerate weight loss, start the day with a psyllium-based cereal such as All-Bran or Bran Buds. Check the labels for content.

BEFORE I LEAVE YOU

It is my sincere hope that you will use these tips to streamline your beauty, not complicate it. Although how you look is important to your overall well-being, it shouldn't dominate it.

Take a tip, use it, and then evaluate it. Did it work for you? Did it make life easier? Was it enjoyable? Was it fun? Did it solve that problem? Did it save you money? Did it make you feel in control? That's what these tips are meant to do. This is what beauty should do for you.

INDEX

A

Absolutely Fabulous, 7

Academy of General Dentistry, 279

accessories, **212–221,** 235: bridal, 186–87; pregnancy, 193

acne, 34, 74: prevention, 17–18; solutions, 18, 119, 294–95

age spots, treatment, 19

airplane food, 284

alcohol, 249: effect on skin, 24

alfalfa, 243

Alley, Kirstie, 266

almond oil, 23, 40, 130, 140, 144

aloe powder, 243

aloe vera, 23, 33, 50, 57, 128, 243, 300

alpha hydroxy acids, 27, 34, 198

Alt, Carol, 248

American Cancer Society, 290

Anbesol, 101

Anderson, Pamela, 264

Aniston, Jennifer, 266

Ann-Margret, 248, 267

anti-intimacy foods, 72

antler tips, 90

apple cider vinegar, 41, 81, 248

Applegate, Christina, 98

apple polish, 132

apricot kernel oil, 23

arms, 260

arnica, 74

aroma therapy, 76

ascorbyl palmitate, 28

aspirin, 246, 295

athletic shoes, 216

attitude, **2–13**

avocado, 127, 144

avocado oil, 23

azulene, 64

B

baby oil, 22, 108

baby powder, 64, 132

baby wipes, 26, 230, 283

bacteria, 78

bag balm, 207

baking soda, 57, 58, 65, 125, 198

balloons, 129

banana, 130, 247
bangs, 136, 142
Banks, Tyra, 265
bargains, 279
bath treatments, 26, 54–58
beauty bashers, 6–7
beauty foods, 82
beauty schools, 279
bee pollen, 87
beer, 125, 128
beets, 280
belly button, 60
belts, 220
benzoyl peroxide, 18, 295
Bergen, Candice, 248
beta carotene, 87
bikini area, 64, 296
biotin, 87
Bisset, Josie, 98
blackheads, treatment, 19
bladder wrack, 68, 243

bleaching, 102, 198
bleeding, 77
blisters, 49, 52
bloat, 57, 74, 84, 88,
    254–55, 261
blood stain removal, 232
blotchiness, 198, 295
blow-drying, 134, 142, 143,
    270, 271
blueberries, 77
blue green algae, 87
blush, 111–12, 120, 177,
    271
body lotion, 283
body-shapers, 258, 262
body types, 159, 257
boots, 209
borage oil, 87
boric acid powder, 35
bra fitting, 69, 291
brassy hair, 133

bread, 249
breast cancer support, 290
breast treatment, 69
breath freshener, 72, 297
bridal beauty, 184–88
bridesmaid attire, 189
brillo pad, 50
broccoli, 96, 247
broken capillaries, 34
bronzing powder, 111,
    117–18, 205, 252, 254
bruises, 74
brushes, makeup, 104
burdock, 243
burns, 35, 77
butcher's wax, 209
butter stain removal, 232

C
cabbage, 96
caffeine, 68

calamine lotion, 294

calcium, 43

callus, 52

Campbell, Naomi, 265

cancer support, 290

capsicum, 243

cardamom, 243

carrots, 81, 247

Carter, Lynda, 266

cashmere, 154

castor oil, 41, 127

cat's claw, 88

cayenne pepper, 77, 243

Cellasene, 68

cellulite, 59, 60, 67–68, 301

ceramides, 28

chamomile tea, 20, 41, 56, 74, 146, 264, 298

cheekbones, 111, 120

cheese, 81

chemical straightening, 147

chemotherapy, 286

chickweed, 243

chitosan, 239

choline, 88

chromium picolinate, 239–40

cinnamon, 243

citrus fruits, 56, 81

cleavage, 254, 259, 301

Cleopatra, 22

closet organization, 224–26

cloves, mouthwash, 66

CNN, 7

coats, 157–58

coconut milk, 21, 199

coenzyme Q 10, 68, 88, 240

coffee, 68, 83, 145, 247, 301: stain removal, 232

cold cream, 16

cold sores, 77, 296

collagen, 90, 92

Collins, Joan, 268

colonic cleansing, 94

colors, 158, 169

comfort, 159

compliments, 6

concealer, 107, 300

conditioner, 62, 63, 278

conjugated linoleic acid (CLA), 240

constipation, 94

control slip, 261

cornmeal, soft skin, 37

corns, 52

corn starch, 36, 51

cortisone cream, 44

cosmetic counters, 11, 276, 280

couture, 152

Cox, Courteney, 265

cramps, feet, 50

cranberries, 77, 81, 146

Crawford, Cindy, 264

crayon stain removal, 233

creatine, 240

crow's feet, 31, 119, 136

cucumber, 22; enlarged pores, 20; eyes, 32; silky skin, 20

curls, 141

Curtis, Jamie Lee, 248

cuticle, 41

D

DAE, 28

dandelion root, 243

dandruff, 127–28, 132, 208, 300

Dang Gui, 88

denim, 155

dental advice, 279

deodorant soap, 206

deodorant, 51, 75, 200, 297: stains, 76

detoxifier, 58

DHEA, 88

diamonds, 218

diet foods, 247

dieting, **304–9**: effect on skin, 24

dishwashing detergent, 295

diuretic, 60

Drescher, Fran, 262

dress casual, 167–68

dress codes, 174

dressing thinner, 258–62

drugstores, 280

drug use, effect on skin, 25

dry cleaning, 234

dry patches, 198, 199

dry skin, treatment, 19, 20

duct tape, 301

Dunaway, Faye, 268

E

echinacea, 89

eczema, 33

E! Entertainment Television, 7

egg, 41, 125, 127, 247, 299

elbows, 23

Elfman, Jenna, 265

elimination, 94–95

emollient, 28

endermologie, 67

ephedra (Ma Huang), 243–44

Epsom salt, 19, 59

eucalyptus, 56, 61, 292

evening primrose oil, 89

excersize: anti-bloating, 255; at work, 168; no time, 273; quick slimming, 253

exfoliant, 28, 57; lips, 27; oily skin, 16

eye: brightener, 61; illness, 288; puffiness, 32, 59, 122, 296

eyebrows, 100–103, 116, 121, 254, 288, 300

eyeglasses, 116
eyelids, 121
eyeliner, 109, 120, 230
eye redness reliever, 18, 294
eye shadow, 104, 108, 120, 121, 131, 170, 177, 296

F

fabrics, 154–55
face lifts, 299
facial hair, 100
fall wardrobe, 204
farsightednes, 116
fatty acids, 95
feet, **48–52,** 61, 76, 208, 260, 301: odor, 51, 75
fennel, 244
fiber, 94
film containers, 283
fingernails, **40–45,** 85, 253, 271–72, 287, 301

fish, 96
flaky skin, 20, 31
flaxseed, 95, 244
flaxseed oil, 23, 89
food: anti-intimacy, 72; beauty, 81; body-detoxifying, 96
foundation, 104, 106–107, 119, 169, 278
fragrance, 70–71, 180, 218
freckles, 35
free radicals, 24
free samples, 276–77, 280
frizz tamer, 271
Fuentes, Daisy, 264

G

gamma-lineolic acid, 89
garcinia cambogia, 240–41
garlic, 75, 81: juice, 18; oil, 45

garlic and papaya diet, 309
garment bag, 225
gas, 74–75
gelatin, 44, 125
Gibbons, Leeza, 265
ginger, 51, 57
gingko biloba, 89
ginseng, 57, 89
glasses, 116
glutamine, 241
glycerin, 28
golf ball, 50
grapefruit diet, 305
grape seed extract, 90
grass stain removal, 233
gravy stain removal, 233
green tea, 244
Griffith, Melanie, 98, 268
grooming, 168
guarana, 244
gymnema tea, 244

H

hair, **120–47**: accessories, 170; as camouflage, 136–37; coloring, 78, 85, 137, 132, 145–46, 147, 194; emergencies, 300–301; fragrance, 70; illness, 289, 291; removal, 63–64; special occasion, 177, 180, 181; treatment, 84–85, 208, 265, 270–71

hair dryer: see blow-drying

hair gel, 300

hairspray, 128, 213

handbag, 175–76, 212–13, 256

hands, **40–45**, 61, 62, 198, 207

hangers, 230

hangover, 76, 297–99

Hatcher, Teri, 262

hats, 235

Hawn, Goldie, 97

hawthorn, 244

Helix shears, 141

hemorrhoid cream, 32, 299, 301

henna, 194

Hewitt, Jennifer Love, 266

HMB, 241

honey, 18, 20, 21, 40, 127, 206

horsetail extract, 35, 195

hosiery, 216–17

humectant, 29

Hurley, Elizabeth, 266

hydrocortisone, 29

hydrogen peroxide, 65

hydroquinone, 32, 35, 198

I

ice cubes, 25

illness, **286–92**

ingrown hairs, 64, 75

ingrown toenails, 52

ink stain removal, 233

insect repellent, 301

Ireland, Kathy, 262

isopropyl alcohol, 29

J

jackets, 156–57

Jell-O, 57

jewelry, 71, 180, 187, 218–20, 228, 235

jojoba oil, 56

Judd, Naomi, 97

juice fast, 304

jump rope, 168, 273

Just Shoot Me, 7

K

kava, 244

kelp, 20, 244

kitty litter, 56

knits, 192, 234

kola nut, 244

kombucha, 90

kvlar fiber, 43

L

lace, 162

lavender, 58, 61

laxative, pore cleanser, 20

L-Carnitine, 68, 241

leather, 154, 163, 233

legginess, 257–58

lemon, 16; age spots, 19; enlarged pores, 34; skin lightener, 21

lemon juice, 125, 296

lentils, 247

linen, 155

lip balm, 44, 280

lips, treatment, 27, 198

lipstick, 112–15, 170, 176, 177, 179, 280, 289, 299–300: stain removal, 233

Locks of Love, 291

loofah, 60, 63, 68, 199

Look Good…Feel Better, 290

Lopez, Jennifer, 265

Loren, Sophia, 267

Lucci, Susan, 266

Lunden, Joan, 262

lycra, 154

M

makeup, 104–22: bags, 227; bridal, 184–85, 188; brushes, 104; corrective, 107, 115–16, 120–22, 272; emergencies, 299–300; hangover aide, 298–99; illness, 286–89; office, 169–70; organization, 226–27, 228; quick application, 177–78, 271–73; seasonal, 200, 202, 204; slimming, 252–53; special occasions, 176–80

manicure, 41–42

marbles, 62

mascara, 105, 110, 119, 278, 300

massage, 62: feet, 49–50

mastectony, bra fitting, 291

matching, 160

mayonnaise, 127

McEntire, Reba, 98

melatonin, 90

menstrual cramps, 54, 88

Meridia, 241–42

metro gel, rosacea, 33

milk: burns, 35; hands, 41; skin, 16, 33, 57, 264

mini meal diet, 305–7

mirrors, 3, 226, 246

moisturizer, 26, 57, 106, 199,

202, 204, 206, 208, 264
mouthwash, 51, 66, 127
MSM, 90
mustard, 57, 301

N

nail fungus, 43
nail polish, 42–45, 230, 278
nail polish remover, 230, 301
nails, see fingernails and
    toenails
nearsightedness, 116
Neosporin, scares, 31
nettle tea, 133

O

oatmeal, 57, 247
odor: home, 71; foot, 51, 75
office to evening, 171
oil stain removal, 232
oily hair tonic, 131
olive oil, 23; dry skin, 19,

199; hand treatment, 40,
    44, 6; hair, 62, 144
omega-3, fingernails, 44
organization, 8, **224–28**
Orlistat, 242
osteoporosis, 96
OXY 10, 280

P

packing list, 282
pageant contestants, 301
pants, 156
panty hose, 180–81, 228,
    231
papaya, 37, 245, 309
paper cuts, 31
para-aminobenzoic acid, 29
paraffin wax: manicure, 207;
    pedicure, 51
parsley, 72, 245
pasta, 247

pear, 130
pearls, 71, 219
pedicure, 48–49, 51
peppermint oil, 56
peppermint tea: bloating 75;
    exfoliant, 21; mouthwash,
    66
Pepto-Bismol, 77
perspiration, 34
petite apparel, 261
petroleum jelly, 29: chapped
    skin, 21; feet, 49, 61–62;
    fingernails, 44; fragrance,
    70; lips, 27, 59, 113, 301
paper cuts, 31
Phillips, Michelle, 267
photography, 188, 259
photosensitivity, 25
phyllium, 245
pimple: see acne
pineapple, 22, 41, 50

pine needles, 57

polysorbates, 29

pores, treatment, 20, 34, 295

posture, 220

potassium, 95

potatoes, 81, 295; eyes, 32, 59

Povich, Maury, 2

powder, 119, 176, 279

powdered milk, 16

Powers, Stephanie, 97

power suits, 168–69

pregnancy, 86, **192–95**

pregnenolone, 91, 242

pressed powder, 279

prints, 162, 193, 259

propylene glycol, 29

protein, fingernails, 43

psoriasis, 33

pubic hair, 64, 78

pumice stone, 52, 234

purse: see handbag

pycnogenol, 91

pyruvate, 242

R

radiation, 286

rash reliever, 295, 296

Reflections Mastectomy Boutique, 291

restaurants, 248–49

rest rooms, 78

retail law, 160

Retin-A, freckles, 36

Roberts, Julia, 266

rolling pin, 301

Romijin-Stamos, Rebecca, 97, 248

rosacea, 33

rosemary oil, 60, 127

rose oil, 57

rose water 20,32, 34, 292

Ross, Diana, 267

royal jelly, 91

ruffles, 162

runway fashion, 162

Ryan, Meg, 265

S

St. John's Wort, 245

saliva, 233, 294

salsa, 238

salt, 294–95

salt water, 18

sandals, 168, 199, 215

scalp, 33, 60, 126, 127–28

scars: concealer, 116; remedy, 31

scarves, 221

scent strengths, 70

Schiffer, Claudia, 264

Scotch tape, 234

scrapes, 31

Sea Breeze, 131

sea salt, 21, 40, 50, 58, 127

seaweed, 91–92

second-hand shopping, 277

selenium, 92

self-esteem, 2

seltzer water, 127

senna, 245

sesame oil, 130

shampoo, 124–26, 278, 283

shark's liver oil, 299

shaving, 63, 74, 295

shea butter, 264

Shields, Brooke, 266

shoe care, 214, 230–31, 301

shoe polish, 231

shoes, 186–87, 213–16,

226, 282

shopping, 153, 277, 280

shorts, 255

sibutramine, 242

silica, 92

skin: illness, 286–87: remedies and treatment, 19–22, 57, 85, 294–96

skin types, 16–17

sleep: aides, 58; treatments, 61–62

sleep lines, treatment, 21

Slim Line Products, Inc., 291

slip dress, 162

smoking, effects on skin, 24

soap, 37

soda can, 171

Sorbitol, 29

SOS locket, 291

soy, 96

soy sauce, 145

spa three-day diet, 307–8

spicy foods, 238

spider veins, 85

spirulina, 92

split ends, 132–33, 300

spoon, 32, 122, 296

spring wardrobe, 199–200

stains, removal, 230, 231, 232–33

static, 129, 140, 207

stearic acid, 29

stevia, 245

stone massage, 62

strawberries: hair mask, 135; toothpaste, 65

stress, effect on skin, 17

stretch marks, 195

style, 10–13

suede, 154, 234

sugar, 128

summer dressing, 163,

202–03

sun: effect on hair, 143; effect on skin, 24

sun exposure, 32, 76, 201

sunflower seed oil, 29

sunglasses, 217, 298

sunscreen, 26, 200

supplements, 86–92, 93

Surgeon's Skin Secret, 208

sweet potato, 247

swimsuits, 203, 234

Swiss Kriss, 20

T

Tabasco, 42

talcum powder, 230

tannic acid, 32

tanning products, 201–2, 205, 296

tea tree oil, 18, 50, 64, 208, 294

teeth, 65–66: whitener, 115, 297

teething ring, 77, 122, 296

Teflon, 43

telephone, effect on skin, 25

television, attitute, 7

tennis ball, 76

textures, 160

thermogenic burn, 246

Tiegs, Cheryl, 248

tipping, 139

toenails, ingrown, 52

tofu, 96

tomatoes, 81; skin toner, 21

toner, 36

toothbrush

toothpaste, 65, 294

Total Woman Boutique, 291

travel, **282–84**

trends, 163

triethanolamine stearate, 29

Trump, Ivana, 248

tuna, 247

turkey, 247

tweezer, 101

T zone, 17

U

udder balm: chapped skin, 21; lips, 27

Uncolor, 147

undergarments, 180–81

urinary tract irritation, 77

V

valerian root, 245

vanadyl sulfate, 92, 242

vanilla, 57, 128

vanity, 4

varicose veins, 35, 195

vegetable shortening, 33, 199, 207

vegetarian diet, 85

Veronica's Closet, 7

vinegar, 45, 51, 125, 145, 230, 245–46

visualization, 3

vitamin A, 25, 86, 296

vitamin B, 86

vitamin C, 22, 87

vitamin E, 27, 31, 44, 75, 89, 127, 296

vitamin K, 35, 74, 90

vodka, 125

W

walnuts, 145

wardrobe building, 150–51: office, 167–69; pregnancy, 192–93; slimming, 258–62

warts, 75, 296

water, 80, 94, 238, 271, 297: iced, 75; test, 135

waxing, 64, 296

wedding gown, 185–86

weddings, **184–89**

weight loss, herbs and supplements, 234–46

Welch, Raquel, 267

wheat bran, 57

wheat germ, 82: oil, 23

whipped cream, 127

white bumps, 31

wigs, 290

witch hazel, 16, 295; dandruff, 127; enlarged pores, 20; varicose veins, 35

wool, 154

working wardrobe, **166–71**

wrinkles, 22, 84

Y

yeast, 18, 61

Y-Me, 290

Yeoh, Michelle, 266

yogurt, 59, 61, 81, 96, 130

Z

zinc, 43, 92

zip lock bags, 227

ABOUT THE AUTHOR

Diane Irons is a leading force in the field of image, health, and fitness. In addition to her own nationally syndicated radio show, she's been featured on *Good Morning America*, *Inside Edition*, *Sally Jessy Raphael*, *Entertainment Tonight*, CNN, *CBS This Morning*, CNBC, *Maury Povich*, *Montel Williams*, *Howie Mandel*, and the Fox Network.